THE
PEOPLE'S
COURT

THE
PEOPLE'S
COURT

HOW TO TELL IT
TO THE JUDGE

HARVEY LEVIN

From cases adjudicated by
JUDGE
JOSEPH A. WAPNER

QUILL, NEW YORK

Library of Congress Catalog Card Number: 84-17761
ISBN: 0-688-03241-9

Printed in the United States of America

First Quill Edition

1 2 3 4 5 6 7 8 9 10

BOOK DESIGN BY JAYE ZIMET

To my parents

PREFACE

Tens of millions tune in daily to watch real-life dramas unfold on the *People's Court* television show. Dozens of the best of these cases have been brought together in this book, which, like the show, will teach you how to protect and enforce your legal rights while providing edifying entertainment.

If you have a mischievous pet, an unreasonable landlord, a defective toaster, a lousy painter, or a turncoat friend who won't repay a loan, this book is for you. Cases like "P.S., I Hit Your Car," "Does Your Dog Bite, Mister?," and "Abuse at the Apartment" will teach you your legal rights, the reasons for the court's decisions, and common mistakes made in preparing and presenting cases in small-claims court. Included are the common legal hassles people care about most, like auto accidents, problems with pets, defective products, personal injuries, neighborhood feuds, and many others.

The way life is, even if you don't have any problems today, it's a good bet you'll have some soon. But when you know your legal rights, and what you can and cannot expect from others, you may be able to keep your problems from turning into legal battles. This book gives you enough information to resolve many everyday disputes *without* going to court.

The laws that you'll read about apply in most states. Some states' laws have certain quirks, but the basic rules of the game are the same everywhere.

All the legal points in the book are illustrated by *People's Court* cases—many of them humorous, some outrageous, but all real. The litigants on the show aren't actors reenacting a procedure. Every case that's heard on the show was originally filed in small-claims court. *The People's Court* employs researchers who comb small-claims-court files in Southern California, looking for interesting cases. Litigants who qualify are asked to present their arguments on the show and to dismiss their cases in small-claims court. In effect, *The People's Court* is binding arbitration. The parties agree to abide by Judge Joseph A. Wapner's rulings.

Many of the litigants contacted want to have their cases heard on the show. Their reasons vary. On *The People's Court,* judgments are settled immediately after the decision; in small-claims court, litigants may have a modest wait before a judgment is rendered. Some defendants find the show attractive because it pays the judgment. But as anyone who watches the show knows, most people aren't just fighting to resolve a dispute—they're trying to make a point. What better way to make a statement about a contractor who didn't do the job, a friend who hasn't repaid a loan, or parent who won't take responsibility for his child's misconduct than to have your dispute heard on television?

In point of fact, most litigants forget the case is on television. The cameras are hidden from view. What the litigants

PREFACE

do see is Judge Wapner, who has had twenty years of experience in resolving lawsuits. Judge Wapner served for over two decades as a Los Angeles County judge of civil and criminal cases. He began his career on the bench with a stint in the municipal court, where, ironically, his first assignment was the small-claims court. This was followed by his assignment to the superior court, where he served as presiding judge. Litigants trust this distinguished jurist, and they generally accept his rulings, favorable or not.

Judge Wapner says that the series can be educational as well as entertaining, because he's given the chance to explain his decisions to the litigants (and to the general public), a luxury for which there's no time in small claims. In this book, it has been possible to provide even more background on the law and the reasons for each decision.

These cases will make you mad, they'll make you laugh out loud, and they'll make you street smart about the laws that affect your everyday life.

—HARVEY LEVIN

FOREWORD

The People's Court is not my first exposure to small-claims court. One of my first assignments as a judge, more than twenty years ago, was small claims.

But even before I became a lawyer, I regularly appeared in small-claims court—as a plaintiff. As an assistant credit manager of a retail jewelry store, it was my responsibility to represent the company in small-claims court.

My first case involved a woman who had purchased a chest of silver on a conditional sales contract. She failed to make her payments, so we sued for the balance due on the contract. The judge in the case was Orfa Jean Shontz. When the defendant brought the chest of silver into court, Judge Shontz turned to me and said, "Mr. Wapner, this lady can't afford to pay the balance due on the contract. You take the chest of silver that she is offering and I'll dismiss the case." That case made an everlasting impression on me, because it was a lesson in fairness. Equity was more important to Judge Shontz than following the letter of the law.

Thanks to my experiences and *The People's Court,* I have never lost sight of the significance and value of small-claims court. The disputes are just as important as the so-called high stakes cases.

Other than traffic court, small-claims court is the only contact most Americans have with our judicial system. Although cases are typically resolved in a short period of time— usually fifteen minutes—that's all it takes for litigants to form their impressions of our judicial system. Win or lose, people must feel they had their day in court; they must believe the judge listened to their side of the story and gave the matter serious consideration before rendering a decision.

Another observation that struck me after the first taping session was the degree of passion with which the litigants presented their cases. Although most cases involve relatively modest sums of money, they often have an important impact on the lives of the litigants. The woman who saved for two years to buy a used car that fell apart, the man whose neighbor demolished their common wall, the customer whose best shirt was ruined by the dry cleaner, all care a great deal about vindicating their position and upholding their rights. Oddly enough, in many cases, individuals with fifty-dollar disputes over faulty products are aroused more than the company president who is sued for $50 million for antitrust violations. *The People's Court* has sensitized me to the fact that the amount of money involved in a dispute often bears no relationship to the importance of the case.

As for televising the cases that I hear, I'm all for it. I have yet to encounter a litigant who felt *The People's Court* would be their ticket to stardom. To the contrary, the litigants al-

FOREWORD

most always forget that the cameras (which, incidentally, are hidden from the litigants' view) are following the proceedings. Virtually everyone who appears on *The People's Court* wants to win. It's the principle involved, not the monetary gain or loss.

The cameras do, however, provide important, incidental benefits. Many of the people who watch the show remember my decisions and my explanations of the law. As such, they're better able to protect and assert their legal rights. When people know what's legal and what's not, they avoid disputes. Or, at least they're able to resolve disputes without going to court. In this sense, I think *The People's Court* has been a boost to the preventive law movement, which encourages people to tend to their legal problems before those problems blossom into lawsuits.

As for cases that can't be resolved without the help of a judge, I think the show has had a positive impact here as well. The first few months of the show, I was dismayed that many of the litigants appeared in court without adequately preparing their cases. Many people would tell me what a critical witness had to say about the dispute in question, instead of bringing that witness or, at the very least, asking the witness to submit a notarized statement. Similarly, some plaintiffs would ask me to award them damages without submitting a shred of evidence substantiating their actual loss.

Now litigants typically reinforce their case with witnesses, notarized statements, repair estimates, pictures, and other evidence that helps me resolve cases more quickly and fairly. My colleagues on the bench, coast to coast, have reported to me that they have observed more thorough, effective presentations by litigants as a result of *The People's Court*.

I am proud to be associated with *The People's Court*. I'm

13

FOREWORD

also delighted that this book is available for people who want to know more about their legal rights. By the time you close the back cover, I hope you will have enough information to help you stand up for your rights.

—JUDGE JOSEPH A. WAPNER

CONTENTS

CONTENTS

DON'T TAKE THE LAW INTO YOUR OWN HANDS...

1

PROBLEMS WITH PETS

Dog bites person
Dog bites other animal
Feline infractions
Animals injured by humans
Intentional injuries to animals
Problems with pet stores
Recoverable damages for injuries to humans
Recoverable damages for injuries to animals
How to litigate pet cases

The People's Court at times resembles a three-ring circus. This is not to suggest that Judge Wapner or his dutiful bailiff, Officer Burrell, loses control over the litigants. But sometimes the witnesses, especially witnesses like Trotsky the dog, Roddy the cat, and Pistachio the bird, can be a problem. This chapter highlights the most common types of pet disputes that have been litigated in *The People's Court*.

DOG BITES PERSON

Every dog used to be entitled to one free bite. Until fairly recently, that rule protected dog owners from Central to Griffith Park, much to the dismay of mail carriers.

Under the free-bite rule, a dog-bite victim wasn't legally entitled to recover damages from the dog's owner if the animal hadn't previously munched on someone. The reasoning behind this rule was that dog owners had no way of knowing their dog was vicious until *after* the first attack. Afterward, however, the owner was on notice, and subsequent dog-bite victims were entitled to sue for damages.

In recent years, however, many urbanized states, notably California, have laid to rest the free-bite rule. "After all," as Judge Wapner reasons, "someone must pay the victim's medical bills—either the victim or the dog's owner." Even if the dog was a perfect gentleman in the past, the owner is in a better position than the victim to prevent doggie misconduct. Therefore, it's only fair to make the dog's owner bear the loss.

Technically speaking, under the current approach, the dog's owner is "strictly liable." In other words, dog owners are legally responsible for their dogs' misconduct, even when they take reasonable steps to thwart an attack. Restraining a dog with a leash, for instance, doesn't exonerate an owner from liability; if the dog bites, the owner pays.

Even in strict-liability states, pet owners fight like dogs to escape liability. One of the more common strategies in *The People's Court* has been "But, Judge Wapner, it wasn't my dog."

In the case of "The Munched-On Mailman," for instance, the plaintiff, a postman, was attacked by a black dog on the defendant's front porch—but the defendant insisted the dog wasn't hers. The plaintiff said he'd just inserted cards and

20

PROBLEMS WITH PETS

letters in the defendant's mail receptacle when a medium-sized dog lunged at him. The plaintiff fell on his rear, hurting his back. The impolite creature then seized the opportunity to bite his arm.

The defendant countered that she didn't own a black dog. When Judge Wapner asked her if she owned a dog at all, she responded, "No, I own a chihuahua." The confused defendant explained that the dog in question had been "hanging around" and pilfering the food she left on the porch for her cat. Furthermore, she had no idea who owned the culprit, she said.

The plaintiff admitted he'd never seen the black dog before the attack. He believed, however, that the defendant was still responsible, since the dog had been on her porch, eating her cat's food.

The plaintiff had the burden of proving that the defendant owned the phantom dog, and because he couldn't, Judge Wapner suggested that the plaintiff was premature in filing suit. He should have investigated to find the animal's real owner. The defendant, explained the Judge, couldn't be held responsible for a dog that happened to wander onto her property. Therefore, judgment for the defendant.

Animals have ways of making their intentions known, and a person who refuses to heed an animal's overt attack signals could be jeopardizing any suit he might file if the animal carries out the threats. In other words, if you wrongly assume the bark is worse than the bite, don't expect the law to sympathize.

In the case of "Does Your Dog Bite, Mister?" a Doberman owner tried to absolve himself of responsibility for his dog's attack on a fifteen-year-old girl by claiming he'd warned her the animal was dangerous. The defendant, who brought his dog to court, said he'd told the girl the dog was attack trained and could be vicious, but she'd approached it in spite of his

THE PEOPLE'S COURT

warning. He said the dog had attacked the plaintiff when she was only about four feet from the animal. Legally speaking, the defendant felt the plaintiff had "assumed the risk" and was therefore responsible for her own injury.

The plaintiff, however, told Judge Wapner that she'd asked the defendant if his dog was vicious, and he'd assured her it wasn't. Nevertheless, the plaintiff said, she decided not to take a chance and began walking away from the animal when it suddenly lunged at her and took a chunk out of her leg. The plaintiff produced a notarized statement from an eyewitness saying the plaintiff had been walking away from the animal at the time of the attack.

Judge Wapner explained that the dog owner had the burden of proving the plaintiff had assumed the risk of being attacked. Since such evidence was lacking, and since the defendant had admitted his dog was trained to attack, the Judge awarded the plaintiff payment for her medical bills as well as the value of her torn jeans.

Another owner's defense in an animal attack case is provocation. A good example of this defense was the case of "The Punctured Postman." In this one, a mailman (poor mailmen!) alleged that he'd been the victim of a sneak attack by a German shepherd, but the dog's owner claimed that the mailman had provoked the attack by stepping on the dog's tail while it was resting. After all, one must let sleeping dogs lie.

Although the owner hadn't witnessed the incident, he said that he'd seen his dog snoozing only minutes before the attack and that he'd heard his dog yip before it bit. But, since the defendant produced no witnesses to support his story, and the plaintiff denied stepping on the dog's tail, Judge Wapner ruled that the defendant had failed to prove his provocation allegation. As a result, the plaintiff recovered damages.

If the defendant had been able to prove that the plaintiff

had provoked the dog, the result might have been different. Had the plaintiff caused his own injuries, why should the defendant be held liable for them?

DOG BITES OTHER ANIMAL

Like humans, animals have tempers and have been known to fight like cats and dogs. When two pets fight and one or both are injured, legal principles similar to those used in personal injury cases determine liability.

Animal cases are inherently more mysterious than human ones. In personal injury cases, the victim and other witnesses can testify about the incident in question. In animal cases, however, often the only witnesses are the pets themselves. In such cases, judges often find themselves trying to think like animals to unravel the clues.

The case of "Who Killed Tiger?" was one of the saddest and most baffling ever litigated in *The People's Court*. The plaintiff in this case owned a two-pound poodle named Tiger, which met with a gruesome end at the paws of two larger dogs.

For three years, the plaintiff had left Tiger with a friend during the day. While the plaintiff worked, Tiger visited happily with Nifty, the friend's dog, who was similar to Tiger in stature and breed.

One day upon returning to her friend's to retrieve Tiger, the plaintiff found a portion of her friend's house in shambles. Furniture had been randomly rearranged, lamps upset, and personal effects broken. And neither Tiger nor her playmate were anywhere to be found.

While looking for Tiger, the plaintiff stumbled on a large brown dog inside the house. Thinking fast, she wrote down the strange dog's license number before it exited through the doggie door into the backyard and vanished.

THE PEOPLE'S COURT

The plaintiff finally found Nifty in the patio area, badly injured. It suddenly dawned on her that the large dog had raided her friend's house and attacked the two little dogs. Also, since the backyard gates were locked, she reasoned that the only way the large dog could have disappeared was by jumping the fence into the next-door neighbors' yard.

The plaintiff went next door and confronted the neighbors' son, who admitted his dog had the same license number as the one the plaintiff had taken down. When the plaintiff saw the brown dog in the boy's backyard, she knew she'd solved the puzzle. Or part of it. Where was Tiger?

It wasn't until two days later that the plaintiff found her dog lying dead in the yard next door to her friend's house, where their dogs were eating the carcass.

Fortunately, Nifty survived, and the neighbors paid Nifty's vet bills. However, they were unwilling to assume responsibility for Tiger. Therefore, the plaintiff filed suit against them in *The People's Court.*

The defendants maintained that Tiger must have burrowed under their fence and into their backyard. Therefore, they reasoned, their dogs were merely protecting their own territory when they attacked her.

The plaintiff believed that the defendants' brown dog must have killed Tiger on the property owned by the plaintiff's friend and then carried the dead animal over the fence. The plaintiff insisted that the defendants' dog must have been able to jump the fence, since all the gates on her friend's property had been locked when the dog disappeared from her friend's backyard. And after all, if the dog could jump the fence, it could carry along a limp two-pound animal.

The legal issue in the case was this: If Tiger was attacked on the property of the plaintiff's friend, the defendants were liable. If, on the other hand, Tiger had burrowed onto the defendants' property, the defendants' dog was justified in attacking her.

In his decision, Judge Wapner explained that the plaintiff had the burden of proof. That meant it was up to the plaintiff to prove that it was more likely than not that her scenario had occurred. In other words, the plaintiff had to tip the scales slightly in favor of her position to prevail.

"I cannot think like a dog," Judge Wapner said. "I don't say that facetiously; I don't know how a dog thinks. It doesn't seem logical to me that if the defendants' dog is going back to the defendants' property, he would stop on the way and pick up a dog that he has already attacked and now wants to eat. It makes me sort of sick to even contemplate such a thing. The only other possibility is that Tiger burrowed under the fence. Since the plaintiff has simply not met the burden of proof, judgment for the defendants."

There have been other animal mysteries in *The People's Court*. In the case of "Who Got Mrs. Lamb's Goat?" the plaintiff, Mrs. Lamb, was suing her neighbor for goat repairs. Mrs. Lamb alleged that the defendant's two German shepherds had attacked Annie, her pet nanny goat. She insisted that she'd seen the defendant's two dogs injure her goat and then run toward the defendant's property.

The defendant insisted that at the time of the goat attack his two dogs had been at home, and locked in the den at that. Furthermore, the defendant produced evidence that at least ten German shepherds roamed that general vicinity.

The plaintiff couldn't effectively rebut the defendant's testimony and was vague in her description of the attackers. Again, because the plaintiff failed to meet her burden of proof, the defendant prevailed.

Unlike Perry Mason—type defendants, animals rarely confess guilt in open court. Judges understand this and will pin

THE PEOPLE'S COURT

the blame on the owner if the evidence is strong enough to lead a reasonable person to conclude that the owner's pet is the culprit. In animal parlance, if it smells like a duck, walks like a duck, quacks like a duck, and looks like a duck, then it's probably a duck. It doesn't have to acually tell you it's a duck for a judge to reach that conclusion.

One way to establish identity is by bringing witnesses to court to support your conclusion. In the case of "Who Got Mrs. Lamb's Goat?," for example, if Mrs. Lamb had brought in witnesses who identified the defendant's German shepherds as the attackers, then she might have met her burden of proof.

Don't be misled into thinking that the more witnesses you bring to court, the more likely it is that you'll prevail. Much depends on what the witnesses say, how they stand up to the judge's examination, and whether they have a bias in favor of one party or against the other.

In one case on *The People's Court,* for example, it appeared that the testimony of the defendant's witness would be the deciding factor. After he testified, however, the plaintiff told Judge Wapner: "Of course he would say that. He lives with the defendant. They're an item." Ultimately, the plaintiff prevailed.

The best witness is one who's a stranger or casual acquaintance of both litigants. In addition, the witness should have nothing to gain or lose from the outcome of the case. For instance, suppose a passerby happens to see the defendant's dog attack the plaintiff's cat. The witness decides to testify in court only because he or she is sick and tired of dogs roaming the streets without their masters. This person would be an effective witness.

Ultimately, a judge evaluates the number of witnesses along with the quality of their testimony in deciding who should win.

PROBLEMS WITH PETS

It may be that you don't need witnesses to prove your case. For instance, if you're able to capture the attack through a camera lens, the picture may be proof of whodunit.

Other evidence can be compelling. For instance, if you find animal fur that matches the coat of the defendant's pet, it may convince a judge that you should prevail.

If you have proof that the defendant's animal has attacked in the past, that may help your case as well. Of course, such evidence is almost never determinative. In fact, ordinarily this type of evidence is rather weak. But if you can prove that the prior attacks occurred in the same area where your animal was attacked, and that the attacker used the same M.O. (for instance, search and destroy), then a judge may give it some weight.

Finally, immediately after the attack you should write down a detailed account of exactly what happened. At that moment, going to court may be the furthest thing from your mind, yet setting down a written account may be the most important thing you can do to solidify your case. It could take months or even years before the case is litigated, and a hazy memory makes for a bad witness. If you present the judge with a written account of what happened, and you convince His Honor that you wrote the account immediately after the incident (which you can do by having your account notorized), your credibility may be enhanced immeasurably.

FELINE INFRACTIONS

Cats are the darlings of the law. While many cities, especially those in urban centers, have leash laws providing that animals must be restrained in public places, nearly all of these laws exempt cats. Feline critters, except for those that are in heat or season, can roam freely on public property. The reason for the exception is that cats are considered natural predators that can best fulfill their biological functions if they're allowed, indeed encouraged, to roam.

(By the way, dog owners *should* observe their local leash laws. Typically, these laws demand that animals be restrained by a leash, chain, or rope that doesn't exceed six feet in length; therefore, if a dog attacks another animal or person while it's wandering about freely, a judge could rule that the violation of the leash law was the legal cause of the attack. Thus, the dog's owner would be liable to the victim.)

While cats' exemption from leash laws allows them the run of *public* property, when a cat damages *private* property the fur can fly. There are arguments both for and against feline liability for damaging private property.

Opponents argue that if you accept the premise that cats should roam on public property for environmental reasons, then how can you expect them to distinguish between public and private property? Once you allow cats to roam, their paws will inevitably touch private ground. Why should the legal system penalize cat owners for damage that we not only expect but encourage? If we want to protect private property from feline trespass, then we should eliminate the exception in the leash law. If we're unwilling to eliminate that exception, then we should simply tolerate any damage that cats cause.

Proponents of cat liability contend that if people choose to own a cat, they should have a duty to exercise some control over their animal. Cat owners aren't *required* to let their pets roam freely; they simply have that option. Therefore, if they elect to exercise the option, they should be responsible for any damage their cat causes. After all, when a cat damages private property, someone must bear the loss, and shouldn't that someone be the person who has the ability to prevent the damage—namely, the cat's owner?

Oddly enough, the judicial system hasn't clearly resolved

this conflict in favor of either the private property owner or the cat owner. Most judges decide these disputes on a case-by-case basis.

In the case of "The Backyard Cat Fight," the plaintiff was suing her neighbor because his three cats had become frequent and unwelcome visitors to her property. The plaintiff said she was allergic to the cats and that, besides breaking out in rashes, she suffered general health deterioration because of their presence. She also claimed that the cats had destroyed her organic garden by urinating in the soil.

There were several problems with the plaintiff's case. For one, she said that the cats were the sole cause of her health problems, yet under examination by Judge Wapner she admitted being allergic to dogs and birds also.

Second, although she claimed to have "caught the defendant's cats in the act of messing up my garden" several times, she couldn't convince Judge Wapner that the defendant's cats were the ones that had caused most of the damage. In fact, the defendant produced evidence that there was "a blight of cats" in the area.

Finally, even assuming that the defendant's cats were the only intruders, pictures of the plaintiff's garden made Judge Wapner wary of her damage claim. The garden, which might have doubled for a garbage dump, gave new meaning to the word "organic."

Judge Wapner began his decision by explaining that the local leash law didn't apply to cats. He suggested that since cats were allowed to roam, it *might* be unreasonable to penalize the defendant because his cats couldn't distinguish between a public park and the plaintiff's organic garden— such as it was.

On the other hand, Judge Wapner said that he would have taken the plaintiff's claim more seriously had she produced evidence that the defendant's three cats were the main source

THE PEOPLE'S COURT

*The cat in question in the case of
"I Taught I Taw a Puddy Tat."*

of damage, especially to her garden. Had she produced photographs, for example, of the defendant's cats repeatedly doing their dirty deed in the plaintiff's garden, Judge Wapner might have awarded some compensation in spite of the lack of a leash law. But as she failed to meet her burden of proof, the defendant prevailed.

Compare the case of "The Backyard Cat Fight" to the case of "I Taught I Taw a Puddy Tat." In this trial, the plaintiff said that the defendant's cat, Mr. T, had eaten Jake, the plaintiff's cockatiel. Interestingly, the litigants, who were neighbors, didn't dispute most of the facts. In fact, the defendant admitted that Mr. T had eaten Jake.

The defendant's defense was that the plaintiff had courted the danger by inviting Mr. T to Jake's house. The plaintiff, however, maintained that Mr. T had sneaked uninvited into her house via a door inside her garage.

PROBLEMS WITH PETS

In his examination, Judge Wapner learned that Mr. T had entered through the plaintiff's storage door on at least three prior occasions. The plaintiff said that she'd thrown Mr. T out on his tail each time, but had taken no steps to make it harder for him to get back in again.

Judge Wapner felt that in this case it would have been easier for the plaintiff to take precautions than for the defendant to curb his cat. Therefore, the Judge found for the defendant.

ANIMALS INJURED BY HUMANS

Even the most cautious pet owners don't maintain a twenty-four-hour vigil to protect their animals from injuries. And, as with humans, accidents do happen. Dogs jump fences; cats are permitted to wander freely. So, when injury results, who bears the loss?

The most common pet injury cases in *The People's Court* involve collisions between animals and vehicles. In such cases, the leash law often determines who should be the victor and who should take a Vanquish.

If a dog is injured while roaming the streets unrestrained, a judge could rule that the cause of the injury was the dog owner's failure to comply with the leash law. In other words, the judge could presume that had the leash law been obeyed, the accident wouldn't have occurred. Therefore, the owner would have a difficult time recovering damages.

Because almost all leash laws make a special exception for cats, if a cat is hit by a car while roaming the streets, the driver can't use the leash law to escape liability.

Although violation of the leash law may be a cause of an accident, it may not be the *only* cause. For instance, in the case of "The Malamute That Wouldn't Yield," the litigants were suing each other for damages resulting from a collision between a malamute and a truck. The truck owner said that he'd been driving below the speed limit when the dog darted out in front of his truck, causing damage to the vehicle. He was suing for truck repair costs.

The dog owner, who was countersuing for vet bills, admitted that his dog hadn't been on a leash, but argued that the "real cause" of the accident was the truck driver's excessive speed. He contended that the driver had been speeding and could have avoided the accident otherwise.

Judge Wapner made it clear from the outset that the dog owner was at least partly responsible for the accident. After all, speeding aside, the accident couldn't have occurred if the dog had been on a leash. But in California, as well as many other states, judges can award damages to reflect the negligence of both parties. In other words, if one party was to suffer $100 in damages as a result of an accident, but the judge held that party 50 percent responsible, the half-negligent litigant would recover $50.

Therefore, in order to recover anything, the plaintiff in this case would have to prove that the truck driver had been at least partly responsible for the collision. In an effort to do this, the dog owner brought his dog to court to show the Judge that it was large enough to be easily visible to an attentive driver. The dog owner might have also been going for dramatic effect and sympathy, since the dog had sustained permanent injuries that made him limp.

But visibility and drama aside, it was the truck driver's speed that was the real issue. Judge Wapner indicated that the defendant could be held partly responsible for the accident if he'd been speeding. The plaintiff said the defendant had been traveling at a speed of forty miles per hour at the time of impact, while the speed limit in the area was only twenty-five miles per hour.

But the dog owner had trouble convincing the Judge of the truck's speed. Initially he said that he'd observed the truck for about twenty seconds prior to impact, and that during that time he'd estimated the truck's speed. However, when Judge Wapner asked him how he knew his observations had lasted twenty seconds, he shrugged his shoulders and admitted he was unsure of the time factor. Judge Wapner snapped his fingers once and asked, "Is that how long it was that you observed the truck before impact?"

The dog owner answered, "No, it was longer."

Judge Wapner then snapped his fingers twice and asked, "Is that how long it was?"

Yes, that was more like it, the dog owner said. Obviously, the difference between two snaps of a finger and twenty seconds is about eighteen seconds.

Judge Wapner felt that the dog owner couldn't possibly have judged the truck's speed in so short a time. Therefore, there was insufficient evidence of speeding on the driver's part. As a result, Judge Wapner ruled that the leash law violation was the *sole* cause of the accident. The driver recovered his truck repair costs, and the pet owner recovered nothing.

In another collision case, "The Hit-and-Run Chopper," the defendant, whose dog had also been unleashed, succeeded in proving that the plaintiff had been partly responsible for the mishap. The plaintiff, a motorcyclist, had struck and killed the defendant's Doberman puppy, and was suing the deceased dog's owner for the cost of bike repairs. The biker argued that if the dog had been on a leash, the accident wouldn't have occurred.

The defendant, a young boy, admitted that his dog hadn't been on a leash. He explained that the dog's leash had snapped apart the day before the accident and that he hadn't had a chance to replace it. But the defendant maintained that the cyclist had been a quarter of a block away when he saw the dog run into the street. The defendant believed that the plaintiff could have avoided the accident.

THE PEOPLE'S COURT

*The plaintiff's motorcycle before the accident
in the case of "The Hit-and-Run Chopper."*

The plaintiff admitted seeing the dog a quarter of a block before impact, but said he'd been faced with two unhappy choices—hit the dog or veer into oncoming traffic.

Judge Wapner ruled that the defendant was partly responsible for the accident because he'd violated the leash law. But the Judge believed that one quarter of a block's notice had given the plaintiff a third option—to slow down or maybe even stop the bike completely. Therefore, Judge Wapner used the comparative negligence doctrine to find the plaintiff one-quarter responsible for the accident and the defendant three-quarters responsible. Thus, the plaintiff recovered three quarters of his repair costs.

Not all animal injuries occur on the highways of life. Most animal injuries, like most human injuries, occur around the home. In fact, people probably don't fall in the bathtub nearly as often as the family cat eats the family bird or the pet puppy swallows a vengeful bee.

In the case of "The Tortoise and the Killer Sod," the plaintiffs' pet tortoises, Lucy, Jan-Jan, and Samson, died as a result of grazing on poisonous sod the gardener used on their newly planted lawn. The plaintiffs lamented that the tortoises, all of which were about twenty-five years old, had been in the prime of life when they passed on, since tortoises commonly live to be one hundred or older.

The plantiffs told Judge Wapner they'd informed the gardener that their pets would graze on the lawn. Therefore, they felt it had been the gardener's responsibility to use nontoxic substances in the planting process.

The gardener vehemently denied that he'd been on notice about the tortoises' grazing. He did admit, however, that he'd seen them in the plaintiffs' yard when he planted the lawn. Indeed, he'd seen them in the general part of the lawn that was being planted.

The gardener explained that nurseries typically mix weed killers with sod. Since the type of weed killer varies with the time of year the lawn is planted, the gardener didn't know which type was in the sod he'd used on the plantiffs' lawn.

Unfortunately for the gardener, ignorance of the lawn is no excuse in *The People's Court*. Judge Wapner believed that the gardener had a duty to inquire into the toxicity of the weed killer before using it. Since he'd made no such inquiry, the plaintiffs recovered their vet bills.

Interestingly, the plaintiffs didn't seek nor were they awarded the value of their tortoises. Since the animals were members of an endangered species and therefore couldn't have been sold, it was impossible to attach a monetary value to them.

INTENTIONAL INJURIES TO ANIMALS

Some people hate cats. Some hate dogs. Some hate animals in general. Sometimes, that hatred gets out of control and people behave worse than animals. There are few things more senseless or reprehensible than the harming of a defenseless pet.

The case of "The BB Gun Murders" involved such a tragic situation. The plaintiff's kittens, Stinkey and Moon, were gunned down without provocation in the plaintiff's own backyard.

The plaintiff said she'd been awakened one morning by "pinging" sounds. When she investigated, she found several BB's on her back porch. Nearby, her kittens lay dead.

The plaintiff believed that the defendant's sons were the culprits. She hadn't actually seen the children shoot their gun that day, but she produced several witnesses who verified that the children had been seen shooting BB's at animals on numerous prior occasions.

The defendant's three children, all under age ten, didn't appear in court. The defendant argued, however, that his children couldn't have fired the gun on the day in question, because it was locked up and completely out of their reach.

The case presented several interesting legal issues. First, there was no direct evidence that the children were the culprits; but Judge Wapner explained that circumstantial evidence could also be used to establish liability. For example, the Judge explained, suppose a housewife bakes a cherry pie and leaves it on the kitchen counter to cool. An hour later, a piece of pie is missing. About the time the woman discovers the missing pie, she sees her son with cherry pie crumbs around his mouth. True, she didn't see her child eat the pie, but circumstantial evidence presents a compelling case that her child is guilty as charged.

Similarly, in the BB gun case, the fact that the defendant's children had been shooting at animals in the past was strong circumstantial evidence. Furthermore, the father admitted that he *did* allow his children to use the BB gun at other times. On that basis, Judge Wapner concluded that the defendant's children had shot the plaintiff's kittens.

The next legal issue was whether the defendant was liable for the misconduct of his children (see the chapter on neighborhood disputes). In some states, such as California, parents are liable only for the willful misconduct of their minor children. Therefore, normally if a child is merely negligent, the parents aren't liable.

In this case, however, Judge Wapner concluded that the facts presented a textbook case of willful misconduct. Therefore, he ruled that the father was legally responsible.

The next legal question was: responsible for what? As the plaintiff presented no evidence of the value of the kittens, she couldn't recover their value. Did this mean that Judge Wapner would award the bereaved plaintiff only the $18 she presented in vet bills?

Well, the Judge awarded the $18 and more. In most states, a statute allows judges to award punitive damages, which serve as punishment for intentional or reckless misconduct, for willful injury to animals. Judge Wapner felt that the father had been extremely irresponsible in allowing his children to abuse their BB gun privileges. To teach the father a lesson, Judge Wapner awarded the plaintiff an additional $500 in punitive damages.

PROBLEMS WITH PET STORES

Pet shops have been the origin of many a *People's Court* dispute. After all, when that doggie in the window comes home with kennel cough or something more serious, someone must foot the vet bills. Should it be the pet shop or the pet owner?

In the case of "Put Puppy to Sleep," the bouncing puppy that the plaintiff bought from the defendant pet store stopped bouncing and started coughing when she got it home. The cough developed into a serious illness and ultimately she had to have the doggie put to sleep. The plaintiff filed suit against the pet shop for the cost of the puppy as well as vet bills.

A representative of the pet shop defended the lawsuit by producing a written contract, signed by the plaintiff, requiring her to take the puppy to a vet within two days of the purchase. This contract stipulated that if the vet determined the puppy was sick, the pet owner would be required to promptly notify the pet shop, which would then take the puppy back and give the customer a full refund. The contract also stated that there would be no refund if the puppy was put to sleep rather than returned.

Judge Wapner asked the plaintiff if she'd read and understood the contract before signing it. The plaintiff admitted that she'd read it and also admitted that she hadn't taken the puppy to a vet for more than a week after the purchase.

Ultimately, Judge Wapner ruled that the contract was binding and the shop should prevail. The judge noted that a pet shop is legally entitled to limit its liability, provided that the liability limitation clause is reasonable. In this case, the judge felt that it was not only reasonable but humane for a pet shop to insist that an animal be returned rather than put to sleep. After all, the pet shop might have been able to have the animal successfully treated.

But not all pet shops are that humane. Take the case of "The Rottweiler Runaround." The plaintiffs bought a Rottweiler puppy from the defendant's kennel, only to discover four months later that the dog had a genetic hip problem— hip dysplasia. They filed suit against the kennel for the cost of an operation that would help the dog function normally.

The sales contract between the plaintiffs and the kennel had a no-refund clause, which the kennel interpreted to mean that defective dogs should be returned. Under questioning from Judge Wapner, the kennel owner admitted that he would have put the animal to sleep. At that the plaintiffs exploded, charging that such a policy was unfair since the pet had "become a part of our family."

Judge Wapner ruled for the plaintiffs for two reasons. First, the Judge said that the kennel's interpretation of the contract was unreasonable. The contract merely provided for a no-refund policy, and the plaintiffs weren't seeking a refund; they wanted to recover the cost of an operation.

Judge Wapner noted that another part of the contract provided: "puppy guaranteed against genetic defects." The Judge ruled that such a guarantee constituted an express warranty, and that the warranty had been breached. He found the damages that the plaintiffs sought were recoverable under the warranty.

In addition to selling animals, pet stores provide a number of services. One of the most common is giving animals flea baths. What happens when an especially sensitive animal is injured while being dipped?

In the case of "The Fatal Flea Bath," the plaintiff brought her cat, L.C., to the defendant's pet shop for an "ordinary" bath. The defendant gave L.C. a flea bath and the cat died shortly thereafter, allegedly from toxic poisoning. The plaintiff felt the source of the toxin was the flea bath formula.

The defendant admitted giving L.C. a flea bath, but maintained it was a common practice to use a flea-killing formula on an animal that had fleas. The plaintiff admitted that L.C. had had "a few fleas."

The defendant said that she'd been using the antiflea solution in question for several months without incident. In fact, nothing like this had occurred in her twenty years of doing pet business.

The defendant brought to court a cat breeder who testified that it was common practice to use the solution in dispute for bathing cats.

Judge Wapner ruled for the defendant, saying that there was no direct evidence the toxin had come from the flea bath. A statement from a vet or an autopsy report would have been helpful, but the plaintiff had presented no such evidence.

But even had the plaintiff produced such a report, she probably would have lost the case. Judge Wapner found that the defendant simply wasn't negligent. It was reasonable to give the plaintiff's cat a flea bath, since the animal had fleas and there were no clear instructions to the contrary. Furthermore, the solution had been used without serious problems by many pet stores. It was a tried and proven product, and a pet shop isn't required to guarantee that an animal won't have an unusual reaction to a safe product. Therefore, sadly, the plaintiff was out of luck.

In another, rather bizarre service-related dispute, the case of "The Pink Pussycat," the plaintiff, a professional photographer, took his white cat to the defendant's pet shop to be dyed blue. Why would anyone want a blue cat? Well, the plaintiff had been hired to shoot a blue-eyed model with cat in hand, and what goes better with a blue-eyed model than a blue cat?

Unfortunately, the cat was dyed pink instead, ruining the photo session. Pink was just all wrong. So, the plaintiff sued for a $25 refund and for the $225 that he'd paid his model for showing up on the day of the ill-fated photo session.

The defendant argued that the plaintiff had been in a big hurry the day he left his cat. The plaintiff admitted he'd been rushed, but said that he'd left his phone number in case the defendant had questions. Furthermore, the plaintiff said he'd

PROBLEMS WITH PETS

The plaintiff and his pink cat being interviewed
after the case of "The Pink Pussycat."

been emphatic that blue should be the color of his true
cat's hair.

The defendant said that she'd been unsure of the desired
color, but thought the plaintiff had said fuchsia. Judge Wapner asked, "If you weren't sure, why did you do the job?"

"Because he had already paid," came the reply.

"And you believed that something was better than nothing?" speculated Judge Wapner.

"Yes."

Judge Wapner ruled that the defendant had been wrong to
perform the job without being certain of the color. Furthermore, the Judge felt that the plaintiff was so insistent about
the color that he must have at least mentioned it at the defendant's shop. The defendant was guilty of a bad dye-job,
and the plaintiff recovered $250.

RECOVERABLE DAMAGES FOR INJURIES TO HUMANS

Once a judge establishes liability on the part of a pet owner, the plaintiff becomes entitled to collect damages. But what damages? What about compensation for aggravation? And how about something for the pain?

Certain costs are never recoverable in a lawsuit—for instance, inconveniences such as taking time off work to file your lawsuit, or time off to appear in court. In personal injury cases, attorney's fees are almost never part of a damage award.

Typically, plaintiffs are entitled to medical expenses, both past and future. In the case of "Bad Dogs and Englishmen," for example, the plaintiff, who'd been attacked by the British

The Judge examining the plaintiff's scar in the case of "Bad Dogs and Englishmen."

defendant's dog, recovered several hundred dollars in basic medical costs. However, the plaintiff also wanted to be paid for plastic surgery to remove an unsightly purple scar the injury had left on her leg.

Even though the plaintiff hadn't yet incurred plastic surgery costs at the time of the lawsuit, Judge Wapner awarded her the expenses. As the Judge explained, the plaintiff was entitled to be "made whole," and that included the cost of scar removal.

In many cases a plaintiff can recover lost wages, but claims for lost wages can get tricky. If, for example, a plaintiff was physically unable to work as a result of a defendant's misconduct, then lost wages would be recoverable. In order to recover lost wages, however, the plaintiff must prove a loss of income. For example, if a plaintiff was unemployed at the time of injury, lost wages wouldn't be awarded. Similarly, if the plaintiff's employer was to pay the salary during the recovery period, lost wages wouldn't be appropriate.

In the case of "The Punctured Postman," the plaintiff was out of work for two days as a result of a dog attack. The post office didn't dock him for the two days; however, he did lose two days of sick pay. Judge Wapner felt that losing sick pay was equivalent to losing salary, and therefore awarded him $160 in lost wages.

A plaintiff may also be entitled to damages for "pain and suffering"—that is, compensation for the throbbing leg that keeps him awake at night or the shooting pains that distract him at work. Of all the compensable items in a lawsuit, however, this is the most complicated, because the value of pain and suffering is difficult to calculate. There are no schedules that show the value of an aching back, no real standard to guide a judge. Judicial discretion usually determines these awards. Often judges calculate pain-and-suffering awards by establishing medical costs and multiplying them by two, two and one half, or three, but awards vary considerably from case to case.

Much depends on the plaintiff's evidence. If you're the plaintiff, probably the most effective way for you to establish pain and suffering is to keep a daily diary—a blow-by-blow account of what you feel as you're feeling it. A diary tends to produce larger pain-and-suffering awards than an after-the-fact summary in court.

In certain cases, judges can award punitive damages. These damages serve as punishment to the defendant for reckless or intentional misconduct. For example, if a dog owner was to order his animal to attack an innocent victim, a judge would almost certainly award punitive damages.

In many cases, the plaintiff isn't sure what damages to seek. For instance, in the case of "The Punctured Postman," the plaintiff sued for more than $600 in punitive damages, but it was established during the trial that the defendant's conduct hadn't been reckless or malicious. Although the plaintiff failed to seek pain-and-suffering compensation, it was also established that the plaintiff had felt discomfort for several days following the attack. So Judge Wapner denied the plaintiff's punitive damage claim, but awarded him $600 for pain and suffering.

At first glance, it may appear unfair for a judge to award damages for something a plaintiff failed to request. But judges have discretion to consider damages that are established by the testimony, even if they weren't formally requested at the time the plaintiff filed his complaint. In legalese, judges may award "damages that conform to proof." It's especially important that small-claims-court judges have such discretion, since most plaintiffs aren't conversant with technical legal theories.

RECOVERABLE DAMAGES
FOR INJURIES TO ANIMALS

When an animal is wrongfully injured, courts award many of the same costs that injured humans can recover. For example, an animal owner is entitled to compensation for vet bills. He can also recover special damages. For instance, suppose a show dog is injured to the point that it can no longer be entered in competitions. If the pet owner could prove a loss of income based on the animal's prior track record, a judge might include that loss in the damage award.

Sometimes pet cases go to court because the defendant believes that the vet bills are out of line with the value of the animal, as in the case of "The Pit Bull and the Pussycat." The defendant's pit bull had attacked the plaintiff's cat, and since the dog wasn't on a leash and attacked the cat on a public sidewalk, Judge Wapner ruled that the defendant was legally responsible for the injury.

But the defendant really wasn't contesting his liability. His contention was that the plaintiff shouldn't be awarded $688 in vet bills. The defendant argued that the cat was worth $50 tops, and it would be unreasonable to require the defendant to pay a vet bill that was so out of line with the value of the animal.

Judge Wapner was both unimpressed and irritated by the defendant's argument. The judge noted that it was "rather callous and insensitive" on the defendant's part to expect the plaintiff to put his cat to sleep and simply buy another one to minimize the cost. As with human awards, the plaintiff was legally entitled to have his cat "made whole." Therefore, the plaintiff recovered the cost of veterinary care.

Don't be misled into thinking that *animals* are legally entitled to be "made whole." There are limits to the legal recognition of an animal's value. After all, under the law, animals

45

are considered property—one of the most difficult legal concepts for an animal lover to grasp. The litigant who cried to Judge Wapner, "But my horse just isn't the same person anymore," probably will never understand Judge Wapner's ruling, rejecting her claim for emotional distress to her horse.

In the case of "Pebbles, the Chicken-Lickin' Poodle," the plaintiff's chickens had been attacked and killed by the defendant's dog. Judge Wapner explained that the most that the plaintiff could recover was $5 for both chickens. That figure represented the market value of the chickens, not the personal value that the plaintiff attached to them. Incidentally, in that case Judge Wapner denied the plaintiff's claim because he was keeping the chickens in violation of a zoning ordinance.

While people are legally entitled to recover damages for the pain and suffering associated with a wrongful injury, pain-and-suffering awards are never made in animal cases. Ingenious litigants sometimes argue that they aren't asking compensation for the pain and suffering their pets endured, but for the agony they themselves felt as a result of their pets' injuries. Nice try, but it won't work.

HOW TO LITIGATE PET CASES

For the Plaintiff

- Bring witnesses or notarized statements from witnesses establishing that the defendant or the defendant's pet was the cause of your injury.
- If your pet was injured, bring photographs of the pet immediately after the injury.
- If you were injured by an animal, bring photographs of the injured area. (Make sure to get the photos taken before the injury begins to heal.)

PROBLEMS WITH PETS

- If you wish to recover for pain and suffering, be prepared to show the judge the injured area, especially if there's a scar. Disregard this point if the injury is in a private area, such as the buttocks.
- If you have a diary describing your pain and suffering while you experienced it, bring it to court. The diary is often a key factor in collecting sizable pain-and-suffering awards.
- Bring all doctor and vet bills, including estimates for future treatment.
- Also bring doctor or vet reports that describe the injury, treatment, and prognosis.
- If you're suing to replace your animal, bring at least two estimates establishing value.
- If your animal is obedient, you may choose to bring it to court. Much depends, however, on the judge. Some judges like animals and may be impressed with your pet. Others may not. Consider this point carefully before you decide.
- If you were injured by an animal and you lost wages during your recovery period, bring documentation from your employer.
- If the attack site is difficult to describe, bring either pictures of the area or a diagram. Use the pictures or the diagram as you explain your case to the judge.
- If you think the defendant will leave his pet at home, bring a picture of the animal if possible. This is especially important if identification is an issue.

For the Defendant

- Bring witnesses or notarized statements from witnesses who support your story.

- If you believe that the plaintiff's medical bills are excessive, obtain notarized statements from medical experts who support your position.
- If the plaintiff is suing to replace a pet and you believe the claim is excessive, bring notarized statements from at least two pet store owners who can attest to the pet's value.
- If the plaintiff is alleging that your animal is vicious and you dispute that, you may wish to bring your animal to court. Of course, only do so if your animal will sit passively during the trial. If this strategy backfires, it can be disastrous.
- If the plaintiff alleges that your animal attacked the plaintiff's pet, consider taking pictures of the plaintiff's animal. This can be effective strategy, especially if the plaintiff's animal is larger than yours. Of course, the pictures must accurately depict size.
- If identification of your pet is an issue in the case, take pictures of animals that look similar to yours in the area where the attack occurred.
- If the attack site is difficult to describe, bring either a picture of the area or a diagram. Use the picture or diagram as you explain your case to the judge.

2

A CRASH COURSE IN MOTOR VEHICLE LAW

Rear-end collisions
Parking-lot mishaps
Lane changes gone wrong
Speed reading
Accident tips

"The other guy" has been responsible for so many accidents that there ought to be a law against him.

If you've been involved in a car accident, you feel uniquely damaged. Your body hurts; your car is crumpled; your life is disrupted. Yet a survey of *People's Court* cases shows that most car accidents are little more than variations on several basic themes.

REAR-END COLLISIONS

Even in childhood, our minds are poisoned about the rear. Bringing up the rear is a distinction without any honor. Being a horse's ass is downright humiliating. Therefore, it should come as no surprise that we throw the book at the driver who brings up the rear in a rear-end collision.

In most states, the "rear driver" is presumed to be the cause of a rear-end accident. The reasoning underlying this presumption can be found in Rules of the Road, Section 11,234: "You must drive far enough behind the car in front of you to safely stop if the other driver does something really stupid."

Although the rear driver is presumed to be the culprit, this presumption can be rebutted. For example, the rear driver might be exonerated if he or she could prove that the accident occurred because the lead driver unexpectedly backed up.

The legal rules for rear-end collisions sound simple enough. Leave it to *The People's Court* to find rear-enders who would give Perry Mason an Excedrin headache.

Consider the case of "The Three-Way Pileup." The plaintiff was a biker whose motorcycle stalled for just "a split second" at a red light. Unfortunately, that was long enough for a car to knock the biker and his girlfriend off his two-wheeler. Sound like an open-and-shut case?

The biker claimed that the car that had hit him was pushed by another car, driven by the defendant. The defendant, however, denied this, saying the car in front of his had hit the biker *before* he hit that car.

The plaintiff, however, offered as evidence a police report that supported his version. The report said the defendant had been inattentive and traveling at an excessive speed at the time of the mishap.

Now, in most courts of law, police reports are considered hearsay, and therefore not admissible evidence in court. After all, in most cases, the police officer who writes the report wasn't actually a witness to the accident, and therefore the account is secondhand at best.

Small-claims judges, however, can bend the rules of evidence for the cause of justice. In this case, Judge Wapner allowed the plaintiff to introduce the police report into evidence, but, because it was hearsay, he gave it less weight than the direct testimony offered.

Judge Wapner believed that the defendant, being at the tail end of the collision, really had no way of knowing whether he'd hit the other car before or after it hit the cyclist. This combined with the police report was enough to lead Judge Wapner to conclude that the defendant had, indeed, caused the accident.

As for damages, the plaintiff sought—and recovered—the cost of repairing his motorcycle. Claiming his bruised leg had caused him considerable pain and several sleepless nights, he also asked for compensation for pain and suffering, and was granted a $50 award.

However, the plaintiff was unsuccessful in his demand for $330 in wages lost as a result of not being able to use his motorcycle to get to work for several days. Judge Wapner explained that the plaintiff could have traveled by either bus or rented car to work. Had he chosen any reasonable alternate means of commuting, he would have been entitled to reimbursement for its cost; because he'd failed to find other transportation and thereby cut his losses, however, he wasn't entitled to be reimbursed for his lost pay.

In a last-ditch effort, the plaintiff argued that he should be able to collect $10 per day as compensation for losing the enjoyment of his cherished chopper. As Judge Wapner explained, however, that claim was more psychic than legal. Therefore, the plaintiff recovered only the $592 it cost to repair his bike, along with the $50 for pain and suffering.

PARKING-LOT MISHAPS

On the surface, it would appear that parking-lot accidents would hardly require the dispute-settling skills of a judge. Most parking-lot incidents involve two cars, one moving and one stationary. It doesn't take an Oliver Wendell Holmes to figure out who's liable in such a case.

Once you scratch the surface (*especially* when you *scratch* the surface), however, you'll realize how difficult these cases can be to prove. Often the culprit flees the accident scene, leaving not so much as a written confession. Therefore, circumstantial (indirect) evidence is often all there is to go on in parking-lot mishaps.

Take the case of "Hit and Run at the High School." The plaintiff alleged that his parked car had been struck by an auto driven by a teenager. The plaintiff didn't see the accident, but several aspiring tennis players did. They jotted down the license plate number of the getaway car, enabling the plaintiff to track down the owner—the defendant.

During the trial, the defendant admitted he had a fifteen-year-old son, but insisted his son hadn't driven the car in question on the day in question. Judge Wapner explained that it was the plaintiff who had the burden of proving it was "more likely than not" that the defendant's son was the culprit.

The eyewitnesses told the judge they'd seen a car of the same description and license plate number as the defendant's overshoot a parking space, hit the plaintiff's car, and speed off. The witnesses further testified that it had been the right front fender of the defendant's car that struck the plaintiff's vehicle. This testimony was critical, since the defendant admitted that his right front fender was dented. Although he insisted his fender had been dented when he purchased the car, his dent proved to match the one on the plaintiff's vehicle. Moreover, the defendant's son fit the rough description of the offender provided by the witnesses.

Judge Wapner concluded that the defendant's son had done the deed. However, the dispute still wasn't resolved: The plaintiff was suing the car's owner, not the owner's son. Under the law of many states, a car owner is liable for damage or injury caused by anyone who drives it, provided the driver had the owner's explicit or implied permission to drive the vehicle.

In this case, Judge Wapner decided that there *was* implied consent. It had come out during the trial that the father left his car keys easily accessible to his son, even though the turbocharged minor had taken them on prior occasions. Therefore, Judge Wapner ruled that the defendant was liable for the cost of repairing the plaintiff's car.

Sometimes, not even a written confession can resolve a parking-lot dispute. In the case of "P.S., I Hit Your Car," the plaintiff testified he'd left his car in the employees' parking lot at work one morning, only to return that afternoon to find it dented and bearing a note. The note contained a forthright admission of guilt by the defendant, so although this wasn't the happiest moment in the plaintiff's life, he felt confident of a swift resolution. Of course, it only happens that way in the movies.

The defendant had a more complicated story to tell. After accidentally striking a parked car in the employees' lot, she said, she had indeed written a note of confession. In her haste to leave, however, she asked the security guard to put the note on the hapless car. Since she'd pointed out the car bearing the mark of her bad driving, she fully expected the guard to carry out her request without any problem. To her dismay, she said, the guard left her mea culpa on the wrong auto.

As proof, she offered the court a notarized statement from

the security guard, who admitted there had been some confusion. Furthermore, she claimed she'd already arranged to pay repair costs to the owner of the car she'd really damaged. Curiously, the owner of that car didn't appear in court.

The defendant's proof that she was dealing in good faith with the other car owner may have cost her the case. The repair estimate she submitted for the car she said she'd really hit was dated prior to when she'd testified the accident occurred. With the defendant's story thus smelling of a parking-lot rat, the plaintiff prevailed.

LANE CHANGES GONE WRONG

You're driving down the freeway when you suddenly realize you must change lanes to exit at a fast-approaching off-ramp. But there's a car in the next lane, close enough behind to make a lane change perilous. Any seasoned driver knows the solution to such a dilemma: With a flick of the old blinker, simply signal the other driver that you plan to change lanes. The driver will either slow down and let you in front, or speed up and get out of your way.

In the case of "The Fourth-of-July Fender Bender," while in heavy Independence Day traffic, the plaintiff found himself in a lane that suddenly merged with the one in which the defendant was truckin' along. As the plaintiff attempted to change lanes, he heard the defendant say, "If you try to get into this lane, I'll tear your car apart, and it won't be the first time I've done it."

In spite of these somewhat discouraging words, the plaintiff tried to merge; however, this merger was less successful than the Wall Street variety—the plaintiff's car was creamed.

The defendant admitted just about everything the plaintiff alleged. His defense was as simple as his motoring etiquette.

A CRASH COURSE IN MOTOR VEHICLE LAW

The litigants describe their accident in the case of
"The Fourth-of-July Fender Bender."

He felt he didn't have any obligation to accommodate the plaintiff, and therefore, tough torts.

Judge Wapner agreed with the defendant, with one exception. The Judge suggested that although the defendant hadn't had a legal obligation to allow the plaintiff to cut in front of him, courtesy dictated otherwise. But a judge sits on the bench of law, not good manners. Judge Wapner explained that the plaintiff had had a legal obligation to wait until he could execute his lane change with reasonable safety. It would have been wiser to stop and wait rather than risk an accident. Therefore, Judge Wapner was forced to rule for the defendant. Nevertheless, no one present felt the defendant was someone they would want to dine with at Chasen's.

SPEED READING

In some states, speed limits are not absolute. For instance, although an area has a posted speed limit of thirty-five miles per hour, you might have the right to drive faster when driving conditions are optimal. Early on a Sunday morning, doing forty-three in a thirty-five-mile-per-hour zone might not be considered a violation of the law. Conversely, when driving conditions are ghastly, you could be ticketed for speeding even without exceeding the posted limit. The designated speed limit is a gauge for safe driving, given typical conditions; you may have a right to exceed it or a duty to drive below it.

Incidentally, because federal law mandates that no one drive faster than fifty-five, partly to save energy, you cannot top that speed on any road under any conditions.

Speeding isn't necessarily the cause of an accident that occurs when one of the drivers is traveling at an unsafe speed; the other driver may be the real cause of the collision. Judges, however, have considerable discretion when it comes to assessing blame. Once a judge determines a driver was traveling at an excessive speed, the judge could rule that the speed demon was at fault, even if he actually was not.

This legal theory of automatic liability is called negligence per se. Under this theory, if someone breaks a law designed to prevent a given type of accident, a judge can automatically impose liability on that person if such an accident occurs. The speeding laws are designed to prevent accidents, so a motorist who becomes involved in one while speeding could be held liable under the negligence per se doctrine.

Critics argue that the doctrine is unfair, because in imposing automatic liability the judge could be overlooking critical testimony and, perhaps, find the wrong person guilty.

Some judges are reluctant to use the negligence per se

doctrine because of its rigidity. Judges do have another option. For instance, in an auto accident case in which one of the participants was speeding immediately before impact, the judge could rule that the speeder has the burden of proving that he or she didn't cause the collision. In other words, the judge would presume that speeding caused the accident, but the violator would have an opportunity to rebut that presumption.

In the case of "Things That Go Bump in the Street," the defendant crashed into a construction worker's air compressor, which was lying on the side of a street.

According to the construction worker, the plaintiff in the case, the defendant was speeding down a residential street where his compressor lay in plain sight, on a clear day. She smashed into the compressor, totaling it, and then drove off in a big hurry. The plaintiff's brother gave chase and finally cornered the defendant at her home.

Had the plaintiff been able to prove that the defendant was exceeding the twenty-five-mile-per-hour speed limit when she compressed his compressor, Judge Wapner could have used the negligence per se doctrine to rule for the plaintiff. But the plaintiff had problems proving his allegation. He estimated that the defendant had been traveling at forty miles per hour when she left the scene of the accident, but he had no concrete proof. As he hadn't been in a vehicle himself when the incident occurred, he was unable to clock the defendant by comparing her speed to his. His estimate was based on his "trained eye," and this wasn't substantial enough to prove his case.

Furthermore, the defendant vigorously disputed that she'd exceeded the speed limit, maintaining she was traveling at a speed between twenty and twenty-five miles per hour at the time of impact. Therefore, Judge Wapner had to evaluate the case strictly on the basis of what had happened.

THE PEOPLE'S COURT

The defendant argued that the plaintiff should have protected his compressor by setting out warning cones. After all, she reasoned, an air compressor is the last thing a driver would expect to hit.

Judge Wapner explained that the defendant might have broken the law by failing to stop at the scene of the accident. The law in California (and many other states) requires drivers to stop and leave all necessary information regarding identification when they're involved in an accident that causes death, injury, or property damage. Failure to abide by this law could result in a fine and imprisonment.

While Judge Wapner explained that he didn't have jurisdiction to hear a criminal dispute, he said that he could consider the fact that the defendant elected to flee the scene. This behavior, according to His Honor, tended to show a "consciousness of guilt." Regardless of the speed limit, Judge Wapner explained, the defendant had a duty to drive carefully. Hitting an object that was visible to the casual observer simply didn't constitute careful driving in the Judge's book.

But the plaintiff also had problems with his case. California law required him to place some type of marker around the compressor. By failing to do so, he too had violated a law.

Many states, including California, allow judges to apportion liability to reflect the fault of both parties to an accident. For instance, if Judge Wapner ruled that both parties to an accident were equally at fault, the plaintiff would recover only half his damages. In the compressor case, Judge Wapner determined that the defendant was 80 percent responsible for the accident, since she hadn't been paying sufficient attention to her driving; the plaintiff, who'd failed to protect his property, was 20 percent to blame. Consequently, the plaintiff recovered 80 percent of the value of the compressor.

A CRASH COURSE IN MOTOR VEHICLE LAW

ACCIDENT TIPS

The term "exercise in futility" must have been coined by a philosopher upon overhearing two bickering motorists at the scene of an accident. Although they can become quite colorful and descriptive, words can't repair a dented door or untwist metal. And fighting won't sway the judge who sits in judgment of the collision.

Difficult as it may be, restraint must prevail at the accident scene. The last thing you need is an assault-and-battery charge—or to be assaulted and battered yourself!

But don't fall to the ground and beg forgiveness either. If you confess guilt at the accident scene, your statement could be used in court to seal your fate. Furthermore, until you have a chance to evaluate what happened, or have a lawyer evaluate it, you're not in a position to determine who's legally responsible for the collision.

Keep a cool head at the accident scene. If the other driver provokes you, resist the temptation to argue or fight back. Bear in mind that sometimes witnesses will offer help to the person who's least offensive; if you're a real pain at the accident scene, you could damage your case as much as your car.

After a mishap, you should spend your time jotting down important information. Make sure you get the other driver's name, address, and telephone number. Also get the driver's license number and license plate number. Obtain the name of the other driver's insurance company and, if possible, the policy number.

People who witnessed the accident could make a dramatic difference if you and the other driver dispute liability or damages. Therefore, get the names, addresses, and telephone numbers of as many witnesses as possible. You may have to be politely assertive, but persistence will pay off.

THE PEOPLE'S COURT

Even the coolest head can be rattled by a car accident. As a safeguard, make a checklist of the information that you'll need in case of an accident and keep it in your glove compartment. There are few feelings more unsettling than waking up in the middle of the night following an accident and realizing that you forgot to take down the other driver's license plate number.

One of the most common problems in car accident cases is piecing together hazy memories for an accurate account of what happened. Although the moment may haunt you, the details will soon escape you. It's especially difficult if the matter can't be resolved amicably; a court trial can take months, even years. Therefore, before you leave the accident scene, make detailed notes recounting the events that led up to the collision. Your notes should include the time, weather, traffic conditions, and locations of other vehicles near the accident scene. You should take special care to note the location and speed of the vehicles that were involved in the accident immediately before, during, and after impact.

In car accident cases, one picture can be worth a thousand litigious words. Therefore, if possible, keep a camera in your glove compartment. You can never be too well prepared. Besides, if the other driver is aware that you know what you're doing, it might give you a psychological edge.

If your car is damaged and you believe the other driver is responsible, get at least two, preferably three, written estimates from auto repair shops. Make sure these estimates include the type of work that needs to be done as well as the price. If the matter goes to court, you'll be awarded the lowest of the three estimates.

If you're hurt in the accident, see a doctor as soon as possible. The longer you wait before getting help, the more difficult it will be to recover medical expenses. Many auto accidents cause soft-tissue damage, especially around the neck area. Soft-tissue injuries normally aren't apparent until a day or two after impact—in some cases even longer. So it's wise not to make a quick settlement; wait until you're sure everything is okay.

If you're injured, you may be entitled to damages for pain and suffering. For instance, if your leg was hurt in a car crash and you couldn't sleep for a week as a result, you might be entitled to damages for your discomfort. Similarly, if your injury resulted in permanent scarring and impairment of your physical appearance, you could recover pain-and-suffering damages for embarrassment or humiliation. Keep a running, detailed diary of any pain or discomfort resulting from an accident. Note the nature of the distress, the time you felt it, and how it affected you. This will help you convince the court that you have a legitimate case for recovering such damages.

Although it's difficult, perhaps impossible, to attach a monetary value to pain and suffering, such awards are common in personal injury cases. Often judges and juries will look at the victim's medical bills as a benchmark for determining compensation. In California, for instance, it isn't uncommon for juries to award three times the amount of the victim's medical bills for pain and suffering.

Furthermore, if a victim misses work because of an injury, lost wages could also be part of a damage claim.

Normally, it's a good idea to try settling the dispute with the other party or the other party's insurance company. However, if you deal with the other insurance company, you may be at a disadvantage: "Low balling" (undervaluing the claim) is too often the name of the insurance game. Therefore, you should consult an attorney before you enter into serious negotiations. Many bar associations offer free or low-cost consultations with a lawyer. For details, call your local bar association and ask to meet with a lawyer who specializes in personal injury law.

THE PEOPLE'S COURT

Finally, if the case is appropriate for small-claims court, be sure that when you appear in court you have your written account of the accident in case you need to refresh your memory, your diary detailing any pain and suffering, medical bills, a doctor's report, proof of lost wages, and estimates for car repairs. Also, bring either your witnesses or notarized statements from your witnesses. Offer the judge any other evidence that appears to help your case.

3

NEIGHBORHOOD FEUDS

Disputes involving trees and bushes
Building walls between neighbors
Kids will be kids and parents will be litigants
Neighborhood noise

Judging from the volume of neighborhood disputes that land in *The People's Court,* you would think civilized society was near collapse. Viewers of the show must have the impression that more people are suing their neighbors than loving them.

Neighborhood disputes are an area where the law and common decency aren't necessarily one and the same. You won't win a lawsuit because your neighbor lacks common courtesy. Nor will you win because he refuses to adapt to your lifestyle.

People have a legal right to live the way they wish, provided that they don't make it *unreasonably* difficult for their neighbors to live in peace and quiet. Reasonableness is the key issue here. If your neighbor throws an *occasional* loud party, you probably have no right to complain. It's when the partying becomes a nightly tradition and you're constantly losing sleep as a result that the scales of justice might come to your aid.

Of course, in taking a neighbor to court, you face the peculiar problem of making bad blood between yourself and someone you're likely to see again. And again, and again. Face it, it's hard to avoid a neighbor, and therefore suing him can sometimes, in the long run, make it more difficult to live in reasonable peace than whatever provoked you to take him to court. Unfortunately, when your neighbor pushes you against the wall, suing may be your only recourse.

DISPUTES INVOLVING TREES AND BUSHES

Self-help is the name of the game when it comes to disputes involving trees and shrubs. These cases are exempt from the parting advice of *People's Court* host Doug Llewelyn: "Don't take the law into your own hands. You take them to court." Many states allow you to sidestep the courts in these matters and take the law into your own hands.

For instance, if your neighbor's tree overhangs your property, you may have a legal right to cut the branches back to your property line. For legal protection, you should inform your neighbor in advance of your intention to do so. Once your neighbor learns the branches present a problem for you, he or she might be willing to do the cutting. If, however, your neighbor is unsympathetic, you could cut them yourself. But *do not cut past the property line*. If you do, you could find yourself on the wrong side of a lawsuit.

Furthermore, in some states, you might also be entitled to

NEIGHBORHOOD FEUDS

cut intruding roots back to the property line—even if you kill the tree in doing so. The law usually provides that a tree must be entirely on one person's property.

Perhaps all of this sounds simple and straightforward enough, but it's been the subject of a number of *People's Court* disputes. Take the case of "Tree over Troubled Neighbors." The plaintiff was suing her neighbor for damages she claimed the neighbor's tree had inflicted on her roof and cars.

According to the plaintiff, the tree had assaulted her property on at least two occasions. Once was in the middle of a rainy, windy night—not the kind that Southern California is famous for. The plaintiff and her husband were awakened by a loud crash and, looking out the window, they saw fallen branches from the neighbor's tree all over their driveway and on their cars, which were scratched and dented. On another inclement night, branches fell onto the plaintiff's roof, poking holes in it and causing a portion of it to cave in, she said.

The defendant's defense was the bad weather. She said the heavy winds and rain on the nights in question made the damage an act of God, for which she could hardly be responsible.

The law allows that no one can be held liable for damages caused by an act of God—that is, by "an inevitable event occurring by reason of the operations of nature unmixed with human agency or human negligence." As the plaintiff in this case presented no evidence of negligence on the defendant's part, and even corroborated the claim that bad weather had accompanied each incident, Judge Wapner ruled that the damage had indeed been the result of acts of God and found for the defendant.

In another tree dispute, the case of "A Walk on the Wild Sidewalk," the plaintiff claimed his sidewalk had been damaged by roots from the defendant's tree. According to the plaintiff, pressure from the tree's rambling roots had torn open portions of his sidewalk, and he submitted photos to back up his charge.

The defendant countered that the guilty tree had been on his property when he bought it. Furthermore, he said, the tree had been present when the plaintiff bought his house. Obviously, the plaintiff had known about the potential problem and had opted to buy the place in spite of it. Why should the defendant be blamed for the plaintiff's bad decision? Besides, the defendant continued, if anyone was held responsible, it should be the former owner.

Based largely on the photos, Judge Wapner ruled that the defendant's tree roots had caused the damage in question. The Judge went on to explain that when a person buys property, he assumes all the rights, duties, and obligations of the previous owner. Since the intruding roots belonged to the defendant, he alone was accountable for them. Therefore, the plaintiff prevailed and recovered $575, the lowest of the three estimates he submitted for repairing his sidewalk.

Trees haven't been the only leafy instigators of lawsuits on *The People's Court*. Bushes have had their day in court as well. And sometimes there has been confusion over what kind of plant was the troublemaker. In the case of "The Bottle Brush Bush," for example, the plaintiffs were suing the defendant for cutting down their trees, while the defendant was countering that he'd done nothing but trim their bushes.

According to the plaintiffs, a married couple, they'd awakened one morning to find their three beautiful, fourteen-foot trees cut down to the six-foot height of the fence separating their property from the defendant's. They produced pictures of the damage. These cherished trees, they mourned, had provided them with privacy and seclusion in the middle of a crowded city. They did admit, however, that some of their beloved branches had overhung the defendant's property.

The defendant retorted that the so-called trees were really

just ugly, overgrown bushes. He said the ivy that grew unattended all over these bushes kept rearing its ugly head
through his fence. As evidence, he presented pictures along
with some ivy he claimed to have cut from his side of the
fence on the morning of the massacre.

The defendant also said that he'd warned the plaintiffs that
the ivy was growing out of its league and had asked them to
trim their vegetation. "You trim it yourself," the plaintiffs had
allegedly replied.

This provoked a heated response from the husband-plaintiff:
"I would never tell my neighbor to 'cut it yourself,' " he said.

"Oh, you're lying," said the defendant flatly.

The defendant felt he'd done everyone a favor by cutting
the bushes down. "I even had to help the trash man clean
up after the trimming," he said, to illustrate his good-neigh-
borliness. "I didn't even finish polishing my Hudson that day."

Judge Wapner told the defendant that he too had once
owned a Hudson, but he refused to let a common taste in
automobiles sway his impartiality. The Judge explained that
the defendant was entitled to use "reasonable care" in abat-
ing (eliminating) the nuisance, which would have meant cutting back anything that intruded onto his property. However,
the defendant had cut every which way—up, down, and
sideways. Since the plants were on the plaintiffs' property,
by cutting the top he'd obviously destroyed branches that
didn't protrude into his yard.

The Judge allowed that if the defendant could have proved
that the plants' height constituted a nuisance, then he *might*
have been entitled to cut the top. But, as no such proof existed, and as the plants—bushes, trees, or whatever—were
ruined, Judge Wapner ruled for the plaintiffs. He awarded
them $750, the lower of two estimates they submitted for re-
placing their whatevers.

In another "bushwhacking" case, "The Hallowed Walls of

Ivy," the plaintiff said the defendant had, in the process of hacking away at the wall of ivy separating their two properties, scratched up his carport. The plaintiff produced receipts for $10 worth of repairs his carport had required following the defendant's unwanted pruning services.

According to the plaintiff, he and his wife were stirred by "a terrible racket" one morning. Running to his driveway, the plaintiff saw "three gardeners chopping away at the ivy" in question.

The defendant said the ivy had been nearly ten overwhelming feet tall before his trimming efforts. It was growing onto his roof, he said, where it was blocking his drainage pipes and loosening his tiles. Therefore, he felt he had every right to trim it. As evidence, the defendant offered a picture showing the overgrown ivy jungle. He claimed that he'd only cut the marauders back to a reasonable height of six feet.

"We have a gardener and so does the defendant," countered the plaintiff, "and both do a good job keeping the ivy trim." The ivy had been a reasonable seven feet high before the defendant brought in his hatchet men, he contended, and posed no problems.

The plaintiff and defendant also disagreed about the location of the ivy. The plaintiff said it was on his property, but the defendant said it was on both properties. The defendant produced pictures indicating the ivy resided on the property line.

Judge Wapner characterized this dispute as a "little war." Why can't neighbors be more neighborly? he asked.

"If one is attempting to abate a private nuisance on another's property," the Judge continued, "he should give notice." However, Judge Wapner felt the trimming had been basically reasonable, since the ivy was causing problems for the defendant, and since virtually all of the trimming was done on the defendant's property.

NEIGHBORHOOD FEUDS

But Judge Wapner ruled that although the defendant had been essentially within his rights in cutting the ivy, damaging the plaintiff's carport wasn't reasonable. Therefore, the Judge ordered the defendant to reimburse the plaintiff for the $10 worth of repairs.

He concluded by asking the two litigants to shake hands in the hallway.

BUILDING WALLS BETWEEN NEIGHBORS

Lawyers like to tell a story about an old man who watched his neighbor erect a large building next to his home, knowing all the while that the building encroached (intruded) on his property by two inches. When the building was complete, the old man demanded $1 million for the encroachment. If he didn't get it, he said, he would sue to have the building removed from his property.

Had this been an actual case instead of an old lawyer's tale, the old man would have had several problems in court. First of all, there's a legal doctrine called laches, which prohibits people from sitting on their rights. In other words, if you know someone is about to violate your rights and you could prevent it but don't, you could compromise any case you might have against the wrongdoer. In the old man's case, he could have told his neighbor about the potential encroachment while it was still easily remedied; because he didn't, his lawsuit would probably be thrown out based on the laches doctrine.

Secondly, even if the builder couldn't prove the old man had been aware of the violation all along, a judge would probably deny the request to have the building removed. Most judges would balance the benefit to the neighbor against the hardship to the old man and award some kind of damage based on the value of the two inches the old man had lost.

69

THE PEOPLE'S COURT

*The defendant presents photos in the case of
"The Willful Wall."*

However, these kinds of cases aren't always as clear-cut as this fictional one. Take the case of "The Willful Wall," which involved a plaintiff who claimed that the defendant had built a brick wall on her property without her permission.

The plaintiff said her problems with her neighbor went back seven years. The week after she moved into her house, she explained, she planted shrubs on what she thought was the property line. The defendant became enraged, alleging the shrubs were on his property. She removed them, at his order, and they died as a result.

The plaintiff also complained that the defendant's ducks and grandchildren had created a noise nuisance for her and the entire neighborhood for seven years.

The plaintiff had filed her lawsuit because of a brick wall the defendant had built the previous year on what he felt was the property line. However, when the plaintiff hired a surveyor to come out and determine who owned what, she'd found that the defendant's wall intruded three quarters of an inch over her property line. So she was suing for the $120 it had cost her to hire a surveyor and the $820 she'd paid in property taxes the year the wall was there. (If you're wondering why she should be entitled to collect her *entire* property taxes, you're right on track.)

Judge Wapner asked the plaintiff in what way the intruding wall had interfered with her property. Had it impeded, for instance, her ability to enter and exit her property?

She replied that it hadn't. But that made no difference, to her way of thinking. The point, as she saw it, was that the defendant had no right to deprive her of her three quarters of an inch of yard.

The defendant chimed in that, when confronted with the surveyor's report, he'd shaved the wall and thereby resolved the problem.

Judge Wapner explained that whether or not the defendant's wall had encroached three quarters of an inch onto the plaintiff's property, the plaintiff was able to show no resulting damage. This seemed to the Judge like a suit based more on spite and revenge than injustice. This day in court was really the result of a seven-year personality conflict, he said. There's an old saying in the law, said the Judge: *De minimis non curat lex.* Literally translated it means "the law does not cure small things." As this dispute seemed to fall well within that area, Judge Wapner ruled for the defendant.

The most common type of boundary dispute involves party walls. A party wall is a wall on the dividing line separating two properties. Under the laws of most states, the people on both sides of the wall have a joint duty to maintain it and, when necessary, repair it. Furthermore, the wall ordinarily can't be removed without the consent of both. When one party fails to fulfill the obligation to maintain the wall, the other can sue for "contribution," or half the necessary maintenance and repair costs.

In the case of "Much Ado About Six Inches," the plaintiffs wanted to build a party wall, but the defendant, their neighbor, refused to share the cost. The plaintiffs went ahead and built the wall anyhow. However, the plaintiffs were now suing their neighbor, alleging that he was using the wall to buttress a slab of cement on his property. Since he was deriving benefit from the wall, the plaintiffs felt he should pay half the cost of erecting it.

The plaintiffs, a husband and wife, said the defendant had told them, "I don't want a wall. . . . Forget it," when they'd approached him about building it. In court, however, the defendant admitted that he was using the wall to support his slab of cement.

When Judge Wapner asked exactly where the wall stood, the plaintiffs replied that it was on their property, six inches from the property line. The defendant, however, maintained that he hadn't known this, that he'd thought the wall was directly on the property line. This six inches, however, was to prove crucial in deciding the case.

Judge Wapner explained that under California law, if someone fences in the other boundaries of his property after his neighbor has already erected a fence on their mutual property line, the neighbor could sue for part of the cost of building the fence (or wall). This is because the person enclosing his property is taking advantage of the fence's presence. It's only fair that people should pay for what they use. But this law didn't apply in this particular case. The defendant had already fenced in the other boundaries of his property before the plaintiffs built their wall.

The defendant, however, still had a problem. By supporting his slab against the wall, he was encroaching onto the plaintiffs' property by six inches. The defendant had no right to use these six inches, even if the plaintiffs had blocked themselves off from them. Therefore, the defendant was trespassing.

However, Judge Wapner decided that the plaintiffs hadn't really suffered any damages as a result of the encroachment. They obviously had no intention of using the six inches anyhow. Therefore, Judge Wapner awarded the plaintiffs only the amount it would cost to remove the defendant's cement slab—$52.

KIDS WILL BE KIDS AND PARENTS WILL BE LITIGANTS

It's a safe bet that no one reading this book was a "perfect child." That term is only used by parents to describe their own kids to infrequent visitors. The fact is no one is perfect—even adults. That's right, every one of us is guilty of indiscretions, some more frequently than others. Why should children be any different from those who set examples for them?

Let's clear the air of some other "minor" misimpressions. Children can be sued. Even a four-year-old tort-feasor (wrongdoer) may have to face the music. Why would anyone sue a child who probably doesn't have ten cents? In many states, judgments are effective for years. In California, for example, a judgment is enforceable for ten years after being issued. A kid might be an acne-ridden pauper on judgment day, but a prince seven or eight years later, and the injured party could enforce the judgment at that time.

Also, in many states, when a child's actions amount to willful misconduct—that is, misconduct that's intentional or malicious—the parents can be held liable along with the child. Many states, however, impose limitations on parental liability. California, for example, limits it to $10,000 per occurrence of naughtiness. Also, parents ordinarily aren't personally liable if their child is guilty of mere negligence.

The case of "The Teenager and the .22" involved a plaintiff who was suing the mother of a neighborhood teen who allegedly had shot a bullet through the plaintiff's wall. She was asking for $220 to repair both the wall and a picture that had been damaged.

The mother/defendant admitted that she kept a rifle in the house for protection, because she and her son lived alone. But she denied she'd known that the rifle was loaded. Furthermore, she maintained that it was her son's friend who'd fired the shot, not her son. How could she be held accountable for what someone else's child had done?

To support her allegation, the defendant produced a notarized statement from her son's friend admitting his guilt in the incident. Her son testified that he'd warned his friend the rifle was loaded, but his friend had just ignored him: "Don't worry" were the friend's famous last words.

Judge Wapner explained that a parent is liable only for a child who engages in willful misconduct, not one who's guilty of negligence. Therefore, if the incident in this case constituted mere negligence, the mother couldn't be called to task.

However, the Judge felt that giving a loaded rifle to a friend did constitute willful misconduct on the part of the defendant's son. Therefore, he found the mother liable for the $220 in repair costs.

NEIGHBORHOOD NOISE

As you've already read, you don't have a right to live in absolute peace and quiet. Noise goes with the territory of city living. For instance, if you were throwing a wedding in your garden, and during the ceremony your neighbor's dog drowned out the "I dos," you probably wouldn't have a legal case, just a case of the blues.

It's when noise is excessive that you may have a case. For instance, if the dog above barked incessantly, then you might have legal recourse. Such excessive noise may constitute a nuisance, and as such, under certain circumstances, you could have the right to use self-help to abate it. However, this is a dangerous thing to do without first checking with a lawyer. If you use too much self-help, you could be sued, just as you could be sued for cutting too much of an overhanging tree.

Before even considering self-help, you should ask your local police department whether there's a specific noise law that's being violated. If so, the police may be able to intervene and solve the problem. Some big cities, for example, have "barking-dog laws" that prohibit excessive barking. If the four-legged offender barks nonstop, perhaps the dog's owner could be fined, and a fine would give the owner an incentive to muzzle the problem.

The defendant in the case of "The Busted Alarm" opted to risk the consequences and stop a neighbor's loudly malfunctioning burglar alarm. As a result, he found himself in the middle of a lawsuit.

The plaintiff in this case claimed the defendant, his neighbor in a condominium complex, had smashed and destroyed a burglar alarm attached to the roof of the plaintiff's unit. He was suing to recover the cost of a new one. The defendant didn't dispute the charge, but felt that his actions had been reasonable. The plaintiff had installed not one, but five burglar alarms—all of which had gone off simultaneously on three previous occasions. Five burglar alarms can make a condo sound like Pearl Harbor revisited, and the defendant felt this amounted to a noisy nuisance. Furthermore, the defendant said, he'd asked the plaintiff many times to control his alarms.

On the occasion in question, one of the alarms either malfunctioned or was set off by the wind; there was no evidence of forced entry. After being awakened by the alarm at eight in the morning and enduring it for an hour, the defendant said, he tried to find the plaintiff, but in vain. So the defendant destroyed the alarm box, restoring peace and quiet.

The plaintiff admitted his alarms sometimes got carried away in the line of duty, but he believed the defendant had helped himself too far in destroying them. He brought a sample alarm to court along with a pillow to demonstrate a less drastic solution. He put the pillow over the screaming alarm box, showing how this simple procedure sufficiently muffled the noise.

Judge Wapner believed that the plaintiff had set himself up for trouble. Granted, crime in Los Angeles is bad, but five—count 'em, five—alarms in one condo? Also, the alarms had already caused problems on three prior occasions.

Examining the incident in question, the Judge felt that the prolonged ringing of the mechanism with no letup in sight indeed constituted a nuisance, entitling the defendant to use self-help. Furthermore, the Judge said that expecting the defendant to stand with a pillow over an alarm until the plaintiff returned home was unreasonable. Judge Wapner ruled that the defendant had had a right to destroy the alarm and ruled for him.

Even though the defendant won his case, he took a big chance in destroying the plaintiff's property. Sometimes actions that seem reasonable during an angry moment seem irrational once the anger subsides. Furthermore, the defendant had to go to court to prove his case, which is not the fun for the litigant that it is for the spectator. And the defendant was running the risk that a judge might not agree that his actions were reasonable under the circumstances.

"It's a good idea to run your proposed self-help remedy by a lawyer, especially when it involves drastic action. Many bar associations offer free or low-cost consultations with an attorney. The first half hour shouldn't cost more than $20, and a half hour could be enough time for a lawyer to pull out a book or two and suggest ways for you to solve your problem and still have the law on your side. The $20 may be more than worth it to avoid a courtroom battle, even if you ultimately prevail.

4

INJURIES: UP CLOSE AND PERSONAL

Domestic brawls
Good Samaritans
Kid fights
Injuries at business establishments
Damages in personal injury cases

Since *The People's Court* opened for business, so many litigants bearing cuts, bruises, and scars have filed through its double doors that viewers must have sometimes wondered whether they'd tuned in to *General Hospital* by mistake.

You might think the last thing a physically injured person would need is a lawsuit, which can be a pain of sorts in itself. But injuries can require medical attention, and doctors don't work for cabbages. Someone has to pay the medical and other expenses that can result from an injury, and frequently the skills of a judge are required to determine who.

Under the laws of most states, a party who's injured by

someone else generally isn't automatically entitled to recover damages. Usually, the injured party must prove either negligence or willful action by the person who caused the injury. Therefore, if someone hurts you by accidentally bumping into you on a crowded street, you might not have legal recourse.

A California law that has inspired similar laws in most other states provides: "Everyone is responsible, not only for the result of his willful acts, but also for an injury occasioned to another by his want of ordinary care or skill in the management of his property or person, except so far as the latter has, willfully or by want of ordinary care, brought the injury upon himself." Translated, this means you're liable not only for injuries you intentionally inflict on someone else, but also for injuries that result from your carelessness; but a judge won't hold you responsible if the injured person acted foolishly and caused his own injury.

DOMESTIC BRAWLS

Many judges are put in the almost impossible position of having to pierce through the personalities and intimate relationships of total strangers and resolve divorce, custody, and other domestic cases fairly. Small-claims judges, however, generally don't even try to probe into such personal areas. They leave that to Dr. Joyce Brothers and others of her ilk. Small-claims judges confine their interest to who is liable to whom when injuries result from a domestic battle. You might say that the small-claims-court judge serves as the referee after the fight.

In spite of their relatively limited involvement in domestic dispute cases, small-claims judges frequently find themselves hearing stories that might have been lifted right out of a Tammy Wynette ballad. Of all the cases Judge Wapner has heard in *The People's Court,* certainly none has been more ready for Nashville than "Is That Any Way to Treat a Lady?" The plaintiff in this one claimed that her ex-boyfriend had struck her during an argument in the parking lot of a tavern. Several of her ribs were broken, and she was suing for $1,101 in medical expenses.

Apparently, the plaintiff had been sitting in the tavern on the night in question, drinking wine and watching her boyfriend of two years make time with another lady. The defendant's story was that he'd downed "a couple of six packs" with his new girlfriend, and that the plaintiff had become angry and hit him. After the striking incident, he and his new friend attempted to leave, but the plaintiff followed them outside and tried to stop him. "She grabbed my right shoulder," he said, "and I accidentally hit her when I swung around."

The defendant relates his side of the story in the case of "Is That Any Way to Treat a Lady?"

INJURIES: UP CLOSE AND PERSONAL

The plaintiff admitted striking the defendant, but said he'd provoked her with inflammatory remarks. A sense of delicacy prevented her from repeating the defendant's remarks to the Judge, but she wrote them down and submitted them into evidence. The plaintiff also maintained that the defendant's parking-lot punch had been intentional.

In his decision, Judge Wapner explained the issue here was whether or not the defendant had committed a battery. The law defines a battery as any willful and unlawful use of force or violence upon the person of another. The term "unlawful" is significant, because there are situations, such as trying to protect oneself from bodily harm, in which striking another person is justifiable.

Given the plaintiff's size and the fact that she was unarmed, the Judge ruled out self-defense as a possible reason for the defendant's alleged punch. The crux of this case, said the Judge, was whether or not the defendant had intentionally struck the plaintiff.

In resolving this issue, the Judge conducted an experiment in his chambers designed to show whether or not the defendant could have used his fist under the circumstances described. He concluded that the way the parties were situated at the time of the striking—the plaintiff with her hands on the defendant's shoulders as he swung around—made it highly unlikely that the defendant could have used his fists. The defendant's avowal that the assault had been accidental seemed more credible to the Judge than the plaintiff's contention that it had been willful.

Furthermore, Judge Wapner felt the defendant hadn't been negligent: It appeared that he'd simply been trying to get away from the scorned and angry plaintiff.

Based on all these considerations, the Judge ruled that the plaintiff had brought the injury on herself; judgment for the defendant.

THE PEOPLE'S COURT

In the case of "The Big Red, Bubbie, and the Vacuum Cleaner," the plaintiff, "Big Red," claimed that her boyfriend had hurt not only her but her poodle, Bubbie, and her vacuum cleaner (no nickname) as well. She was suing for $319: $144 for chiropractic treatment, $125 for veterinary services, and $50 for vacuum cleaner repairs.

Big Red alleged that her boyfriend, the defendant, had become violent when she threw him out of her house; she recounted that during their farewell, the defendant had tried to take back the vacuum cleaner he'd given her. "I sat on the vacuum cleaner so that he couldn't take it," she said, "and he kept jerking at it with me on it." She claimed her bucking-vacuum-cleaner ride had aggravated a chronic back condition.

Under the law, if someone wrongfully aggravates a preexisting condition, that person is responsible for any resulting

"Big Red" and Bubbie of the case of
"Big Red, Bubbie, and the Vacuum."

damages even if he didn't cause the preexisting problem.

The plaintiff also said that her dog's back had nearly been broken trying to defend her, and that the vacuum cleaner had been damaged as well.

The defendant claimed that, in the first place, the cleaner was his. He said that he hadn't traded it to the plaintiff for a bike and a lawn trimmer as she alleged. He also said that the dog had been injured when the plaintiff jumped on his back and tried to kick him; she missed him, he said, and hit the dog.

Judge Wapner felt that the issue here was not who owned the vacuum cleaner, but whether or not the defendant's actions constituted a battery. He believed the defendant might have touched the plaintiff, but not forcefully or intentionally. Furthermore, the Judge held that the plaintiff could have avoided injury by exercising good judgment and not sitting on a moving vacuum cleaner.

As far as the dog and the wounded vacuum cleaner were concerned, the plaintiff presented no proof that the defendant had harmed them; they could certainly have been harmed by some other means during the melee described. Therefore, the Judge awarded no damages to the plaintiff.

Domestic injury cases are shockingly common and often result in much more tragic consequences than the two above. Anger always rages strongest against those you're most involved with; as the aphorism points out, "You always hurt the one you love." When an unfortunate domestic situation gets out of hand, try to talk it out before it explodes. If you can't do it on your own, seek professional help. Perhaps the only thing worse than being hurt by someone you love is hurting someone you love.

GOOD SAMARITANS

Suppose while walking on the beach one sunny afternoon, you suddenly spot someone drowning in the ocean. Do you leave the poor, struggling soul to meet fate among the sharks and seaweed, or do you take the dive?

Most of us like to think that the vast majority of mankind wouldn't hesitate before trying to help. But, until recently, the law didn't support our altruistic ideals. Those Good Samaritans who inadvertently made a bad situation worse were sometimes sued for their inadequate heroism. If you tried to save a drowning swimmer and caused him to take in too much water by saving him incorrectly, you might, until fairly recently, have been sued by the victim or the victim's estate. Thus, the law deterred a lot of well-meaning citizens from getting involved.

Recognizing that this was hurting society, many states have enacted "Good Samaritan laws." These laws basically protect Good Sams from lawsuits if they unintentionally cause injury to victims they're trying to help—even if they act negligently. Presumably, these laws have given them carte blanche to show their stuff.

But the Good Samaritan laws haven't altogether ended Good Samaritan lawsuits. Sometimes, the *Good Samaritan* decides to sue after being injured during a rescue attempt. The plaintiff in the case of "The Toga Party Rumble," for example, claimed that the defendant had stabbed him while he was trying to break up a fight. He was suing to recover medical costs, as well as pain-and-suffering damages.

According to the plaintiff, he and his wife had been leaving a party when they heard the defendant and another man arguing. The plaintiff said that when he'd approached them, hoping to calm the situation, the defendant grabbed him. The plaintiff pushed the defendant away. According to the plain-

*The plaintiff submits evidence in the case of
"The Toga Party Rumble."*

tiff, the defendant fell, then got up, and stabbed the plaintiff
with his knife. The plaintiff also alleged that the defendant
had been drunk. And Henry Kissinger thought he had it rough!

The defendant countered that he didn't "think I had anything to drink" at the time. He said the plaintiff and his friends
had bullied him, throwing him to the ground twice and kicking him before he pulled out his pocket knife. He claimed
he'd been in fear of his life and had only been protecting
himself.

But Judge Wapner explained that even if the plaintiff had
provoked the defendant, California law allows people to use
deadly force only if they, or a relative, are in imminent danger of great bodily harm, and deadly force is the only means
of eliminating the imminent danger. Since a knife is a deadly
weapon, and the swing of a knife is deadly force, the defendant would have been entitled to use the knife as he did

only if his life had been in immediate peril. Judge Wapner didn't believe that it had been. Therefore, ruled the Judge, regardless of whose story was correct, the defendant was liable for the plaintiff's injuries because he'd willfully used deadly force in a situation that didn't warrant it.

The plaintiff was awarded $564 for medical costs and $1,000 for pain and suffering, which he said had lasted more than six weeks.

The plaintiff in the case of "The Unrewarded Hero" was also a Good Samaritan. He'd put out a fire at the defendants' house, but had been burned in the process. The plaintiff felt that he'd been burned a second time when the defendants refused to pay his medical expenses, so he was suing to recoup $750 worth of medical bills.

According to the plaintiff, he'd been visiting his girlfriend, who was babysitting the teenage defendant, when a fire broke

The plaintiff shows his injuries to Judge Wapner
in the case of "The Unrewarded Hero."

out in the kitchen while the teenager was attempting to make French fries. "We were in the living room," the plaintiff said, "and heard a burst in the kitchen. We ran in and saw a pan fire. While putting it out, I received burns."

Neither the young defendant nor his mother, who was also a defendant, denied the plaintiff's account of what had happened, but both maintained that the poor manner in which the plaintiff put out the fire had caused his injuries. It seemed the plaintiff had put the burning pan under water to quench the flames. "Anyone with common sense knows you don't put water on a grease fire," said the mother. "You put a top on it and smother it."

Even though this Good Samaritan probably couldn't be sued for any damages he might have caused in his honorable line of duty, he couldn't recover damages either unless it was found that he'd acted reasonably in the face of the emergency. Therefore, in resolving this case, Judge Wapner had to decide whether or not the plaintiff had acted as a reasonable person would have under similar circumstances.

After considering this case, Judge Wapner decided that, given the heat of the moment, so to speak, the plaintiff had indeed reacted reasonably. He also decided that it was the son's negligence that had caused the fire. Thus, Judge Wapner found that the son was liable for the $750 in medical costs.

As for the mother's liability, Judge Wapner explained she could only be held liable for her son's willful misconduct. Although he'd failed miserably as a chef, he hadn't willfully engaged in culinary misconduct. Therefore, the mother wasn't held legally responsible.

Although these two Good Samaritan cases both involved people whose professed good intentions proved harmful to them, you should by no means be discouraged from showing the right stuff in a crisis. These cases demonstrate that the law is usually on the side of those who answer the call—and so are society and your conscience. Find out if there's a Good Samaritan law in your state. If not, and you think there should be, you might want to let your state representatives know how you feel. It could be a step toward a better society.

KID FIGHTS

Adults frequently react with horror to the cruelty children display toward one another: their teasing and ridiculing, their selfishness, their lack of loyalty and gratitude. Where do they get it from? Imagine if adults behaved that way!

Kids who get into trouble can find themselves leaving *Romper Room* behind for the courtroom, even when their misdeeds are directed toward other children instead of adults. Children's fights in particular, because they can be so vicious, frequently wind up before a judge's bench; and the judge might throw the book at junior perpetrators, whether they can read it or not. Furthermore, the parents of pint-sized wrongdoers might also be on the hook when the misdeeds of their offspring are willful.

The People's Court has hosted its share of kiddie disputes, some of which have involved adult-scale injuries. The father and son plaintiffs in the case of "Loaded Backfire," for example, were suing the father of a boy who they claimed had hit the son in the head with his schoolbag, which contained a heavy wrench. They were seeking to recover $190 in medical expenses.

The son/plaintiff, an eleven-year-old, said that he'd accidentally struck the defendant's son, a twelve-year-old, in the face during a game of dodge ball. The defendant's son, he recalled, became angry and issued the old "Meet me after school" challenge.

INJURIES: UP CLOSE AND PERSONAL

The defendant's son hadn't waited until after school, however. He kicked the plaintiff in the shin as they were leaving the lunchroom, the plaintiff said. The plaintiff kicked him back, and the defendant's son grabbed his backpack and struck the plaintiff over the head with it.

The defendant's son tearfully told his version of the story. He said the plaintiff had approached him in the lunchroom, called him a traitor, and started kicking him. "I told him four times to stop," he said. "I tried to walk away, but he kicked me and made me trip. As I got up, I swung my backpack in self-defense. There *was* a wrench in the pack, but I had totally forgotten about it."

The plaintiff countered that the defendant's son's story wasn't true. "He kicked me first," he maintained.

Judge Wapner first noted that a parent is only liable for a child who's guilty of willful misconduct; children alone are liable for damages that result from negligence. In this case, since the plaintiffs were suing only the parent, they could only recover damages for willful misconduct.

"I see no willful misconduct here," continued the Judge, "only what I'd call 'boys will be boys.' I don't think the defendant's son stopped to think about the wrench." Therefore, judgment for the defendant. Judge Wapner called the children before the bench and made them shake hands.

The case of "The Pizza Parlor Punch-out" involved two teenage boys, co-workers at a pizza parlor. One boy had allegedly hit the other, breaking his nose and his watch. The plaintiff was suing his co-worker's mother to recover medical bills totaling $250.

The plaintiff said that he'd arrived at work one day sporting a new haircut that apparently wasn't to the liking of the defendant's son. In fact, the haircut provoked the defendant's son to question the plaintiff's masculinity, and a little verbal combat ensued. Later, as the two boys "were folding

The plaintiff explains what happened in the case of "The Pizza Parlor Punch-out."

pizza boxes," said the plaintiff, the defendant's son "pushed me with the box and said, 'Look how small you are.' I said, 'You can't beat me. I'm strong.' "

The plaintiff said that after this exchange, he'd gone to the restroom to comb his hair, and when he returned the defendant's son "grabbed me from behind, turned me over, and punched my nose."

The defendant's son denied punching the plaintiff. The injury occurred during a wrestling match following an argument, he claimed. The defendant's son brought along a witness who testified that the accused wrongdoer never punched the plaintiff.

Judge Wapner, however, believed that the broken nose and the other testimony, which painted a picture of the defendant's son as a bully, indicated that he had indeed punched the plaintiff. Furthermore, the Judge felt that the punch had constituted a battery—that is, that he had intended to cause injury.

As mentioned above, parents are often responsible for their minor children's willful misconduct. Therefore, the Judge ordered the mother of the wrongdoer to pay the plaintiff $250. Let's hope this inspired the mother to use her maternal influence to make her son check his ornery ways.

INJURIES AT BUSINESS ESTABLISHMENTS

It's true that most accidents happen at home, but they can occur almost anywhere. There you are, walking down the aisle of a supermarket, calmly checking the price of canned tuna, when you slip on a banana peel and land flat on your back in someone else's shopping cart. As you wipe the egg goop from your aching behind, the second word that probably pops into your mind is "sue."

A lot of people don't realize that merchants aren't liable for every accident that occurs in their business establishments. On the contrary, the laws of most states limit merchant liability to only those injuries that result from neglect. Thus, only if the supermarket above wasn't being patrolled adequately and the banana peel had been languishing on the floor for an undue amount of time would a court award you damages. If you slipped and fell thirty seconds after someone dropped the peel, a court would probably find that the store wasn't negligent. After all, it would take a reasonable person more than thirty seconds to detect and eliminate the danger.

The key to merchant liability is reasonableness. Supermarkets and other businesses open to the public must be reasonably patrolled to ensure safety, because accidents in such establishments are foreseeable; but it's unreasonable to ex-

THE PEOPLE'S COURT

*Doug Llewelyn discusses the decision with the plaintiff
in the case of "The Run-Over Roller Skater."*

pect a store owner to find and correct every potential danger immediately.

A roller-skating rink is, perhaps, one kind of business where accidents are inevitable, and, sure enough, at least one skating-related accident has rolled into *The People's Court.* In "The Run-Over Roller Skater," the plaintiff claimed that she'd been bumped by a drunk skater. Alleging that the guards at the defendant's skating emporium had been negligent in allowing a drunk skater on the rink, she was suing the owner.

The plaintiff said she'd seen the wayward skater maneuvering erratically on the rink for an hour before the accident. His behind had touched as much floor as the wheels on his skates had. Judge Wapner asked the plaintiff if she'd alerted the management to the potential danger.

"No," she replied, "but I have told them in the past to be careful. I work in the Los Angeles Alcoholic Center, so I know what I'm talking about when I say the man was drunk."

The defendant countered that he always had at least one guard per hundred customers on duty. On the night in question, he said, there were only twenty skaters and he still had a guard present. The guard and the cashier on duty that night testified that the daredevil skater hadn't seemed drunk to them.

Judge Wapner felt there was insufficient evidence that a reasonable rink staff would have detected that the skater was drunk. Had he been so ripsnorting drunk that it was obvious to anyone, then maybe the rink would have had a duty to keep him out. But the plaintiff simply hadn't met her burden of proof that this was the case. On the contrary, the cashier, who'd come in close contact with him, said she never smelled alcohol on his breath. Apparently, even if the skater was drunk, it wasn't obvious. Therefore, judgment for the defendant.

DAMAGES IN PERSONAL INJURY CASES

Even if you prove someone wrongfully injured you, you could end up in the ironic position of having won the battle only to lose the war, unless you understand what types of damages are recoverable and you're prepared to prove that you're entitled to them.

Medical bills associated with an injury are normally recoverable. Of course, you must prove to the judge that the medical expenses relate to the injury for which you're suing. Therefore, medical reports can be crucial evidence. Also, have your doctor make notes about your injury.

You may also be entitled to future medical expenses, if you'll require additional treatment after your court appearance. However, you'll have to offer the judge hard proof, such as a doctor's statement, of how much those future expenses will be; merely speculative medical expenses that you don't substantiate aren't recoverable. And remember, once you sue, your day in court is over. You can't sue more than once for the same injury.

In addition to medical bills, you can also sue for the pain and suffering associated with the injury. As explained in the chapter on auto accidents, this is an inexact form of damages, because it's difficult to attach a monetary value to pain and suffering. Is a minute of moderate pain worth $5 or $500?

In some big cities, lawyers will tell you the rule of thumb is to double or triple the medical costs to arrive at the damages for pain and suffering. This formula, however, isn't binding on a judge or jury. To maximize the amount of pain-and-suffering damages, it's a good idea to keep a detailed diary during your recovery. Every time you hurt or feel discomfort, memorialize it. The more descriptive, the better. A judge will find your diary more convincing than your foggy memories.

If you lose work as a direct result of an injury, you could recover lost wages. However, you can't recover wages lost while making visits to your doctor or wages lost for time spent in court. The only compensable lost wages are those that result from time missed at work because you were physically unable to perform your chores.

As explained in the auto accident chapter, however, claims for lost wages cannot be speculative. You must prove to the judge that you weren't paid during your period of incapacity. And you must prove how much you would have made had you been working. If you were unemployed immediately before the injury, for instance, and had no job prospects in sight, you couldn't recover lost wages.

If your injury was caused by willful misconduct, many states would allow you to collect punitive damages. Like pain-and-suffering damages, punitive damages aren't subject to precise measurement.

Punitive damages are designed to teach wrongdoers a lesson. Therefore, if a wrongdoer is of modest means, you may recover only a modest amount, since that may be all it takes to teach him or her a lesson. If the wrongdoer is a multi-millionaire, the amount of punitive damages presumably would be larger.

There may be other damages you could collect in a personal injury case. For more information, call your local bar association. Many bar associations offer free or low-cost consultations. Half an hour with a lawyer could tell you how to prepare your case, and also what evidence you would need to prove your damage claim.

5

A LESSON IN LEASING

Security deposits
Rights of landlords
Evictions
Rights of tenants

The cliché "A man's home is his castle" has been translated in different ways by *People's Court* litigants. Some of the most popular translations have been:

- Homeowners are entitled to privacy.
- Homeowners may use necessary force to protect their property and family from harm.
- Homeowners can use their property in any manner they choose, provided they don't cause harm to others.
- Get offa my lawn.

A LESSON IN LEASING

The home-castle metaphor makes sense when one person is unquestionably entitled to possess and use a given property. But the moat muddies when a property owner rents out his castle or any other space to a tenant. After all, both landlord and tenant have legal rights. The landlord owns the property and is entitled to protect it from harm, while the tenant is entitled to use the property without interference by the landlord. Given the inherent conflict, the landlord-tenant relationship is often a battle waiting to happen.

SECURITY DEPOSITS

Both landlords and tenants have moaned to Judge Wapner about the unfairness of security deposits. Tenants complain that they must ante up big bucks just to provide their landlords with peace of mind; landlords groan that this so-called peace of mind often proves woefully inadequate when a tenant goes on a rampage. Indeed, each side has a point, which makes the security deposit a real bugaboo.

Is the landlord required to refund the tenant's deposit if the property is left the way it was found? Does the landlord have legal recourse if a security deposit doesn't cover all damages? These questions sound a bit dry, but dry matter often fuels fiery disputes. Security deposit flare-ups have been among the most explosive cases seen at *The People's Court*.

Until recently, security deposits could be nonrefundable. Tenants could pass the white-glove test with flying colors and still lose their security deposits. The reason for this seeming unfairness was that landlords typically had their tenants sign leases explicitly making these deposits nonrefundable. A deal being a deal, the tenant was out of luck—and refund.

But some state legislatures have recently taken the term "security" to heart. *Webster's Third New International Dictionary* defines "security" as a pledge "to make certain the

97

fulfillment of an obligation." *Black's Law Dictionary* defines "security" as "protection, assurance, indemnification." Nowhere is the term defined as "nonrefundable."

As a result of this startling revelation, some states now prohibit landlords from permanently depriving tenants of their deposits. These states require landlords to return a tenant's deposit, unless:

1. The tenant has damaged the apartment unit.
2. The tenant is behind in paying rent.
3. The landlord needs to clean for the next tenant.

In any case of the three cases listed above, a landlord can deduct the expenses from a tenant's security deposit. Otherwise, upon moving out, the tenant is entitled to a full refund.

In the case of "The Boarder Who Got Bounced," the tenant moved out only three weeks after moving in. The landlord refused to refund the tenant's security deposit, claiming that the tenant had drilled holes in the ceiling. According to the landlord, it would cost her $85 to repair and paint the damaged ceiling. Since the tenant's security deposit was only $80, she decided to call it a wash.

But the tenant was outraged. The nerve, said he, to suggest that it would cost $85 to fill in a few holes. So he sued her for the $80 deposit.

In security deposit cases, the landlord or landlady has the burden of proving the extent of damage and should submit at least two repair estimates as proof. Typically, judges award the lower of the two.

In this case, the landlady failed to obtain even one estimate. In a more formal judicial forum, she would have lost the case based on her failure to produce the necessary evidence, but small-claims judges are often more lenient toward litigants. After all, they're mostly laypeople, and it would be unfair to expect them to know about legal technicalities like the burden of proof.

Nevertheless, a party without proof is like Perry Mason's courtroom without a guilty person to confess: Something essential is missing.

As Judge Wapner has explained many times, when parties don't present proof, it puts him in a bind. If someone has been damaged but fails to present evidence of the cost of damage, the judge can deny the entire claim. But if he does, the wrongdoer will get off the hook because of a legal fine point. And that doesn't seem fair.

If, however, the judge simply takes the word of the party who was injured, that too could lead to injustice. For instance, what if the landlady in this case had asked for $1,000?

As a middle-ground approach, small-claims-court judges have the discretion to "ballpark" a party's damages, provided they have a basis for arriving at a figure.

In this dispute, the ceiling was only twelve feet by twelve feet. In view of his experience as a homeowner and a handyman, Judge Wapner didn't believe it would cost $85 to repair the ceiling. The Judge felt the going rate was more like $40. Since the landlady had retained the entire $80 deposit, Judge Wapner awarded the tenant $40.

There's no such thing as a free lunch, or a free room. If a tenant fails to pay rent, the landlord may retain an equivalent amount from the tenant's security deposit. That's certainly one of the most straightforward laws. The problem isn't understanding the law, it's figuring out who paid what to whom.

A good case in point was that of "The Frat Boys and the Young Landlady." This dispute concerned a California landlady and two Eastern college students. The landlady claimed that she never received the entire $500 that the bi-

*The defendants submitting evidence in the case of
"The Frat Boys and the Young Landlady."*

coastal scholars had agreed to pay for the month they stayed
in her apartment. She said a $250 security deposit and $250
toward the rent were all she ever got. Because the boys never
paid the other half of the rent, she felt entitled to keep the
deposit to cover it.

The frat boys, however, insisted they *had* paid the remain-
ing $250 of their rent. They claimed they'd placed it in an
envelope and left it snuggled up on a bed pillow when they
departed the premises.

Ordinarily, the landlord or landlady has the burden of
proving entitlement to withhold a tenant's security deposit.
This case, however, was complicated by the issue of
payment.

How could the landlady prove that she *hadn't* been paid?
Indeed, how can anyone prove a negative? Because of the
landlady's impossible position, Judge Wapner decided that

the tenants in this case should have the burden of proving they *had* paid.

Of course, the most effective way of proving payment is to produce a canceled check. The students, however, said they'd paid in cold cash, which left them out in the cold. Because they couldn't prove payment, Judge Wapner ruled for the landlady.

Tenants are required to leave an apartment in the condition in which they found it, although they won't be penalized for reasonable wear and tear. If it's filthy when the tenant moves in, it can be just as filthy when the tenant moves out. If, however, a tenant finds a unit spanking clean and leaves it downright dirty, the landlord can use the tenant's security deposit to cover cleaning costs.

For instance, in the case of "The Actress and the Beverly Hills Landlord," the landlord retained his tenant's security deposit because he said her apartment had been left filthy;

The actress and the Beverly Hills landlord react to Judge Wapner's decision.

the stove and refrigerator were grimy, overstuffed garbage bags were randomly scattered about the apartment, and the place generally looked like a B movie—pretty lousy.

The tenant, an actress, countered that the place had been as clean as Doris Day's mind. She even produced a witness who assured the Judge that her friend's kitchen floor could have doubled as a dining-room table.

To withhold a security deposit, landlords have the burden of proving that they need to clean the unit for the next tenant. Ideally, the landlord should produce pictures of the mess the tenant left behind. But in this case, there was no such proof—on either side.

The landlord, however, had hired a cleaning crew to sanitize the vacated unit. Furthermore, he produced a bill outlining the cleaning charges. Judge Wapner felt the landlord wouldn't have incurred that expense if it hadn't been necessary; otherwise, why lay out the cleaning money? Therefore, judgment for the landlord.

In many states, landlords are prohibited from demanding exorbitant security deposits. Typically, landlords who rent out their units on a month-to-month basis are prohibited from requiring more than two or three months' rent as security. But that amount may prove hopelessly insufficient when a tenant does a number on an apartment unit.

The landlady in the case of "Madness at the Mansion," for example, claimed that her tenant's measly $150 security deposit would barely unscratch the surface of the damage the tenant had caused to her hardwood floors. She said the tenant and her furniture had scraped the floors to the tune of $1,000 worth of repair work. What's a landlady without enough deposit to do? Sue the tenant, of course.

This particular tenant, however, was rather floored by her former landlady's allegations. She vehemently denied having marred anything. In this case, as in others of this sort, the

A LESSON IN LEASING

landlady had the burden of proving her claim. This meant convincing Judge Wapner that the floors were badly scarred and the tenant was the culprit.

In court, a picture that shows the damage is the next best thing to being there. The landlady produced pictures, but they weren't very convincing. In fact, if there were scratches on the floors, they were only enough to offend the sensibilities of *very* keen eyes.

Judge Wapner explained that California law required him to award "damages that are reasonable." He felt that the scratches were so minor, if existent at all, that the floors wouldn't have to be refinished. As mentioned before, the doctrine of *de minimis non curat lex,* which literally means "the law does not cure small things," keeps the law out of trivial problems. This was a very small thing, even for small-claims court, so the landlady lost out.

RIGHTS OF LANDLORDS

Residential leases are almost always drafted by landlords. Most tenants believe a lease is a predetermined, ironclad document that can't be modified. And many landlords feel the same way. Once their lawyers draft a "standard" lease, they believe it should stand like the Rock of Gibraltar.

Now hear this: All leases are open to negotiation. Landlords can tailor the provisions of a lease to their needs and so can tenants.

In the case of "Not with My Boyfriend, You Don't," a young lady tried to tailor her lease to suit needs that her landlady found objectionable. Wanting to set a proper tone for tenancy, the landlady had included a "morals clause" in the lease. This clause would have made the lease highly unattractive to Frank Sinatra, Dean Martin, and Burt Reynolds. It prohibited smoking, drinking, and overnight "guests."

THE PEOPLE'S COURT

At first, the tenant agreed to the lease, but later found that Cupid had other plans for her. Shortly after moving in, she began allowing her boyfriend to spend the night.

The Baptist landlady confronted her passionate tenant with an ultimatum: Live by the Good Book, or live somewhere else. The tenant decided she would rather switch lodgings than fight for love.

The landlady, however, felt cheated. After all, the tenant had agreed to the lease, and then beat a hasty retreat without giving any notice. So the landlady sued her former tenant for one month's rent.

In many states, when a landlord and tenant agree to a month-to-month lease, it can only be terminated by giving written notice thirty days in advance. Tenants who move out without first giving such notice could be on the hook for thirty days' worth of additional rent.

In this case, the tenant tried to convince Judge Wapner that the landlady had given up her right to thirty days' notice by issuing an ultimatum. For this reason, the tenant felt she shouldn't be liable for the disputed rent.

Judge Wapner, however, failed to agree with the tenant. He concluded that the landlady hadn't ordered her tenant to move, but rather gave her an option: Abide by the terms of the lease or move. Since the tenant had elected not to live up to the lease, she should have given thirty days' notice.

Although landlords can include special clauses in a lease, they sometimes unintentionally overlook topics that can prove important. When a dispute arises concerning an issue that a lease fails to cover, the law often has to step in and determine who's entitled to what. Many leases, for instance, fail to specify what happens when a tenant improves an apartment unit. When the tenant moves, who gets to keep the improvements? Is the landlord ever required to pay the tenant for these improvements?

A LESSON IN LEASING

In the case of "Abuse at the Apartment," the tenant moved into an apartment with green shag carpeting that might have made even Liberace wince. The tenant removed the green shag and replaced it with the more chic, industrial-gray variety.

When the tenant moved, she removed the carpeting. After all, the tenant reasoned, she'd paid for it and therefore should be able to take it with her.

The notion that you can't take it with you applies to more than just Broadway plays and death; it applies to residential leases as well. As Judge Wapner explained, good taste notwithstanding, the tenant had made several unfortunate choices in her decorating scheme. First, she failed to save the green shag, shabby though it was. The tenant had no right to dispose of the landlord's property and, in doing so, was guilty of conversion—the wrongful taking or detention of personal property.

Furthermore, under the laws of many states, tenants aren't entitled to remove fixtures when they move out of an apartment unit. The lawbooks are full of cases regarding exactly what constitutes a fixture. Traditionally, a fixture was something that couldn't be removed from a building without causing substantial damage. A dishwasher, for instance, was considered a fixture.

Under the more modern legal theory, the intent of the parties determines whether or not an item is a fixture. In this case, Judge Wapner noted that the carpeting the tenant had installed wasn't an area rug but wall to wall. It was cut specifically to the dimensions of the apartment unit and affixed to the floor. For this reason, Judge Wapner decided that the tenant had intended the carpet to be a fixture of the apartment; therefore, the tenant had no right to remove it when she vacated the unit.

While the law provides some specific guidelines for resolving disputes that might arise concerning improvements, unfortunately it neglects other landlord-tenant problems. Take the case of "The Terrified Tenants." This one involved a couple who signed an eighteen-month lease on a Los Angeles apartment unit, only to decide to cut their stay short when the building proved hazardous to their health.

Upon returning home one day, the couple found their kitchen window wide open. Not taking this as a sign that an uninvited visitor might be lurking about, one of the tenants picked up the kitchen phone to make a routine call. Suddenly, she heard a strange voice uttering "the most crude and obscene things I'd ever heard." To their horror, the tenants realized that the voice was coming from an extension phone in another room of their apartment! This might have provided a good opening for an Alfred Hitchcock movie, but the couple decided not to stick around for the shower scene. They fled the building, and so did their confidence in living there. Shortly, thereafter, they moved.

The landlord sympathized but sued, since he felt the tenants had broken their lease without legal justification. The tenants felt perfectly justified, claiming there had been thirty-two burglaries in the immediate area within a month of their own brush with danger. They maintained that the landlord was legally responsible for providing them with a secure apartment unit. Furthermore, they said the landlord had refused their request that he install new locks on the doors and windows.

The landlord countered that he'd told the tenants they could reinforce the existing locks if they wished, but only at their own expense. He believed that security in the building was adequate and that he shouldn't be held legally responsible for the crime problems of Los Angeles.

For his part, Judge Wapner felt that this case was a sad commentary on the state of contemporary urban life. However, he noted, the law doesn't make landlords the insurers of tenants' safety. The landlord, he said, had provided what was expected of him—an apartment unit with ordinary locks. He wasn't required to take extra safety measures because of the burglary rate in the immediate area. Furthermore, the lease contained no specific promises of security. Therefore, Judge Wapner ruled that the tenants hadn't been justified in breaking the lease and awarded the landlord the rent he'd lost during the time the unit had remained vacant.

EVICTIONS

At the end of each session of *The People's Court,* host Doug Llewelyn warns viewers: "Don't take the law into your own hands; you take 'em to court."

Nowhere does this creed apply more than in the area of evictions. We would live in utter chaos if a landlord were entitled to terminate a tenancy merely by changing the locks on an apartment unit and tossing the tenant's belongings into the street.

Fortunately, all of our states have empowered judges, not landlords, to decide eviction cases. And if a tenant has a binding lease, he or she is protected from eviction during the period the lease is in effect, as long as the tenant doesn't violate its terms. Even when a landlord has a seemingly cut-and-dried reason for evicting a tenant, such as failure to pay rent, the landlord must still take the case to court.

Typically, the eviction process begins with a landlord's giving a tenant three days' written notice to either comply with the lease or move out. Technically speaking, this is called a notice to quit. If the tenant is still in violation of the lease when the three-day period has expired, the landlord can then file legal eviction papers in court.

After the landlord files the papers, the tenant files his and the case is set for trial. Should the judge decide that the landlord is indeed entitled to evict the tenant, the judge orders the tenant to vacate within a specified period of time. If the tenant fails to comply, the landlord can summon the help of a marshal to forcibly remove the tenant.

Charles Bronson pictures aside, when a landlord takes the law into his own hands, he leaves himself wide open for a lawsuit. For instance, if a landlord changes his tenant's locks without going through the proper procedures, the tenant could sue for trespass, invasion of privacy, and punitive damages. Vigilante landlords beware!

The problem in many eviction cases is that, human nature being what it is, a feud often ensues after the landlord says he wants the tenant out. With so much fighting going on, it sometimes becomes unclear whether the tenant moved voluntarily or was forced.

Consider the case of "The Boarder Who Got Bounced." The tenant in this one moved out only three weeks after moving in—and not by choice, she claimed. She said the landlord had forcibly evicted her without first going to court. Although the landlord hadn't changed the locks, according to the tenant, he'd snarled that he would make things "very nasty and uncomfortable" if she didn't mosey along. Fearing for her belongings and safety, she moved. This, she said, was an eviction of sorts, since she'd been intimidated into leaving.

The landlord pooh-poohed the tenant's allegations and countered that he was entitled to keep her deposit because she'd neglected to give him thirty days' written notice as required by her month-to-month lease.

The tenant believed her *coup de grâce* was the fact that the landlord had changed the locks after she moved. Didn't that prove, she asked, that she'd received the boot?

The landlord admitted changing the locks after her departure, but claimed he'd only done so because the "frightened" tenant had threatened to return to rip off some of the contents inside. When Judge Wapner asked the tenant if she'd indeed made such a statement, she could only reply: "Not exactly. I said that he's lucky. I'm not a vindictive person because if I was he'd be missing a lot of his precious belongings."

Now, had the landlord made it perfectly clear that the tenant's safety would have been imperiled by continuing to live in the building, then Judge Wapner might have ruled that this was an instance of "constructive eviction." Constructive eviction occurs when the landlord's actions have the practical effect of eviction, i.e., they result in the tenant's being forced to move. A ruling of constructive eviction would have entitled the tenant to damages.

But Judge Wapner felt that not only was the landlord's statement vague, but so much bad blood existed between the two parties that he could only conclude the tenant had moved voluntarily to escape such unpleasant living conditions. The Judge felt there was a mutual agreement to call the lease off. Therefore, the tenant was entitled to a security deposit refund.

RIGHTS OF TENANTS

A State Department strategist might call landlord-tenant law a "zero-sum" game, because a landlord's legal gain is often his tenant's loss, and vice versa. Actually, leasing laws draw a useful series of lines designed to keep landlord and tenant out of each other's hair—and rights.

One line the law draws that's particularly beneficial for tenants is the one that protects their property. A landlord who oversteps this line might be headed toward a courtroom, as in the case of "The Illegally Parked Washing Machine " The

The plaintiff pleads her case in the case of
"The Illegally Parked Washing Machine."

landlord in this case disposed of a tenant's washer, which he claimed had been illegally parked in the tenant's carport.

The tenant admitted signing a lease that provided the carport would be used exclusively for the parking of autos. Still, she protested that she paid rent for the carport as well as her apartment and should be entitled to put anything there she desired. She also protested that her landlord had had her washer towed without any warning. "Even if I'm wrong," she lamented, "the landlord could have come to me . . . then maybe I would have moved it." She further contended that she'd been storing her machine in the carport only temporarily, until she could have it installed in her unit.

Judge Wapner ruled that the lease did indeed provide that the carport space could be used only for motor vehicles. But although Judge Wapner felt the terms of the lease were clear enough, he had problems with the landlord's solution.

The landlord, explained the Judge, had had a couple of options. He could have filed an eviction action against the tenant for violating a term in the lease, or he could have sued the tenant for any damages he might have suffered as a result of the misplaced washer. Unfortunately for him, the landlord's options didn't include taking the law into his own hands. Confiscating the washing machine constituted conversion—the wrongful taking of someone else's property. The tenant might have lost her washer, but the landlord was hung out to dry. Judge Wapner awarded the tenant $175, which was the value of the washing machine at the time it was wrongfully appropriated.

The People's Court has witnessed cases in which the misappropriation was more extensive—cases like "The Ticked-

*The defendant checks the evidence in the case of
"The Ticked Off Tenant."*

Off Tenant." The landlord/defendant in this case rented a room in his house to the tenant/plaintiff, then kicked him out and refused to return his belongings.

The defendant said the plaintiff had deserved to be thrown out, because he was frequently intoxicated and had beat her son with a belt. She said she couldn't continue living with the plaintiff because she was afraid of him. She also claimed the plaintiff had borrowed $650 from her and that she was withholding his furniture only in lieu of repayment.

Looking less than formidable, the plaintiff arrived in court in a wheelchair, although he admitted he hadn't been in one when he lived with the defendant. The plaintiff denied having borrowed money from the defendant, who had no I.O.U. or canceled check to prove she'd made the loan. She claimed the loan had been made in cash.

Judge Wapner, however, ruled that, loan or no loan, the defendant had no right to withhold the plaintiff's belongings. Contrary to the popular saying, possession isn't even close to nine tenths of the law. Besides, a landlord is almost never entitled to confiscate a tenant's belongings, even if the tenant is delinquent in rent. And, as we've seen, a landlord can evict a tenant only by going through the proper procedures.

Also, in this case, the Judge noted that the landlady was abusing her position to remedy a dispute that had nothing to do with the lease agreement. If the landlady needed assistance in recovering her loan, she should have sued for it.

The Judge found the landlady guilty of conversion and ordered her to return the plaintiff's furniture. He also ruled that, as there was no evidence of a loan, the defendant wasn't entitled to any repayment.

Another right guaranteed tenants by the law of most states is the right of "quiet enjoyment." This means that the tenant has the right to use the premises without the unreasonable interference of the landlord. Although landlords have some

A LESSON IN LEASING

rights to protect their property from damage, they can't ride herd on their tenants to the point of making life miserable for them. As the term suggests, tenants have a legal right to live in reasonable peace.

Take the case of "The Sad Swede." The Swedish plaintiff in this case and her son had moved into the defendant's house, where they'd all lived together as one big, *un*happy family. The tenant had paid rent through June 1982, but said she'd been forced to move on June 11 because the landlady/defendant had made life impossible. Claiming that the landlady had attacked both her and her young son, she was suing for reimbursement of the rest of her month's rent.

The landlady countered that the son had acted like a monster. When he wasn't busy playing with steak knives, he'd amuse himself by breaking things around the house. The landlady also said that the tenant hadn't even tried to discipline her budding recalcitrant.

The tenant responded that she had controlled her child, and that the landlady had shown no self-control. She said the landlady's physical attacks on her son and herself had been inappropriate and unjustifiable.

To decide this one, Judge Wapner had to determine whether the defendant had really made the plaintiff's life unbearable. During a thorough interrogation, the landlady was suspiciously evasive. For instance, when Judge Wapner asked, "Did you strike her son?" the landlady replied, "Well, not really, but he was a bad boy. I had to take a hammer and steak knife away from him many times. He would break things."

When the Judge asked the landlady if she'd hit her tenant, the child's mother, she again answered, "Not really."

Finally, the Judge asked, "Do you have a bad temper?"

"I cannot allow a little boy to take a hammer," she said. "I feel this little boy should have a little punishing. . . . The next chance I have I will do it."

Judge Wapner translated these answers as guilt. He concluded that the defendant had indeed played "Landlady Dearest" and, in doing so, had violated the plaintiff's right of quiet enjoyment. By attacking the tenant and her son, the defendant had constructively evicted them. In other words, by imperiling the tenant's safety to such a degree, the landlady had effectively thrown them out on the street, leaving the tenant no option but to move. Therefore, the tenant/plaintiff was entitled to recover the unused portion of her rent.

One real bugaboo in landlord-tenant law is the right of the tenant to have exclusive possession of the premises during the lease. This right isn't absolute. In many states, a landlord does have the right to enter for certain reasons: in case of an emergency such as a gas leak, to make necessary repairs, to show the unit to a prospective tenant, or to show the unit to a prospective buyer of the building. But the landlord isn't entitled merely to make spot checks to make sure the unit is okay. Furthermore, the law in many states requires that, except in emergencies, the tenant be given reasonable notice—usually twenty-four hours—and entry be made during normal business hours.

In the case of "The Tattletale Plumber," the landlady/plaintiff made an illegal sneak inspection of the tenant/defendant's apartment after receiving a harrowing report concerning the unit's condition from a big-mouthed plumber who'd made some repairs on it. Freaked out by the plumber's report of shocking-pink walls and two cats with shocking toilet behavior, the landlady entered the unit unannounced, gasped in disbelief, and took some pictures. She later filed suit against the tenant for the cost of restoring the unit.

In court, the tenant claimed that she'd actually improved

114

the condition of the apartment. She also claimed the land-lady had given her permission to repaint it.

The landlady denied ever having given such permission. Besides, she said, no landlady in her right mind would have approved pink walls.

Judge Wapner explained that whether the walls were pink, orange, or purple, the plaintiff had had no right to enter the tenant's unit for an inspection. The tenant's right to exclusive possession had clearly been violated. He added that the tenant could have been entitled to damages for invasion of privacy had she been able to prove she'd suffered damage as a result of the landlady's actions. The tenant, however, hadn't filed a countersuit.

As for the landlady's lawsuit, Judge Wapner ruled it "was prematurely filed." The landlady, he explained, might have a right to sue once the tenant moved out—if she could prove at that time that the tenant had violated the lease by damaging the unit or altering it without authorization.

In the last five years, the right of families with children to rent apartment units has become a prominent legal issue. Some landlords want to exclude children from their buildings because they believe kids are noisy and destructive, and create problems for other tenants. These landlords feel they have a right to rent to whom they please. Furthermore, they argue that this is an issue vastly different from racial discrimination—it's a matter of lifestyles. If they want to maintain a certain type of environment that will attract certain tenants, why shouldn't they be allowed to?

Unfortunately, it's become increasingly difficult for families with children to find decent housing, especially in urban areas. These families frequently have to pay more for less—a punishment, they say, for being parents. They're particularly irate over the gross generalizations that underlie the landlords' thinking; not all kids are noisy, destructive, and undisciplined—certainly not theirs. They maintain that the landlords' stance amounts to the exclusion of a whole class of people, a class to which, ironically enough, every landlord once belonged. This, the families say, is wrong.

Some state legislatures have sided with the families and prohibit discrimination against families with children.

The People's Court has seen its share of these cases. In the case of "Rosemary's Baby," for example, the plaintiffs claimed that the defendant had refused to rent them an apartment because the wife (Rosemary) was pregnant.

After sending in an application for the apartment, the husband followed up with a call to the defendant, who asked outright if Rosemary was pregnant. The husband acknowledged that she was. The defendant responded candidly that she wouldn't allow children in her building, because it had

*The litigants await Judge Wapner's decision
in the case of "Rosemary's Baby."*

A LESSON IN LEASING

been an adults-only building for a long time and her other tenants wanted to keep it that way. So she refused to rent to the plaintiffs.

The defendant admitted to Judge Wapner that she wanted an adults-only building. She catered to tenants ages fifty to sixty, she said, and they all went to bed at nine o'clock. At their age, the last thing they wanted was to be awakened for two A.M. feedings.

"I'll admit, I don't want an infant," she said to the Judge. "A year-old child wouldn't be as bad as an infant. You have no control over an infant. You can at least slap a one-year-old down."

Nice lady.

Judge Wapner ruled that there was no question that the plaintiffs had been rejected because the wife was pregnant, and that this was a direct violation of a 1980 California law prohibiting landlords from discriminating on the basis of "age, parenthood or pregnancy." This law establishes damages at three times the cost of one month's rent. Because the rent was $500, Judge Wapner awarded the plaintiffs $1,500.

Incidentally, Rosemary gave birth to a boy.

6

SHODDY GOODS

Warranties
Inspections
Buyer abuse
Fraud
Product liability

Inflation combined with what many consider the decreasing quality of manufactured goods has provoked a new age of consumerism, one that offers the buyer more protection than ever before. During the last twenty years, state legislatures around the country have passed a number of consumer protection laws designed to guard against shoddy workmanship and rip-offs. Of course, as legal involvement in the marketplace has increased, so has the number of lawsuits involving defective products.

This chapter explores issues every buyer and seller should be aware of regarding defective products, warranties, inspections, and fraud. You'll probably be able to relate to a lot of these cases. Some may even bring back painful memories. But don't get a migraine all over again about that air conditioner you bought last summer that thought it was a heater. Just settle back, relax, and prepare to become a better consumer in the future.

WARRANTIES

You win a little, you lose a little. Products today may not be as sturdy as when they were made by hand and with care, but the law has compensated by giving consumers certain types of warranty protection.

A warranty is basically a seller's guarantee that a product will either perform or hold up in a certain way. For instance, a seller's promise that a product will last for sixty days without any problems constitutes a warranty. And if the product doesn't live up to the promise, the seller usually has to either fix it so it will or replace it with one that does. A warranty can be written or oral, but obviously a written one is preferable. An oral warranty could end up a matter of your word against the word of the seller, and in court you would have the burden of proof. So, again, it's always best to have it in writing.

The most common type of warranty dispute results from the guarantee's being too vague. A seller might promise, for instance, that a product is the best of its kind, but what exactly has he guaranteed? And how can you make such a warranty stick in court? Promises like "It's in excellent condition" and "You're going to love it" are equally difficult for a judge to fathom.

Most small-claims-court judges—and other judges as well—don't even construe such vague statements as warranties. These claims are mere puffery. It's expected that salespeople will make a pitch to buyers, and their hype shouldn't be taken as a warranty.

If, however, a salesman promises that "you're going to love this product, and if you don't I will give you a complete refund," that's a different story. In this case, it's perfectly clear what the salesman is offering.

When you venture into the marketplace, if you hear something from a salesman that *sounds* like a warranty, but you're not sure, it probably isn't one. You must pin the salesman down and get a specific promise in writing. Only then will you be able to enforce the agreement if the product doesn't stack up.

The plaintiff in the case of "The Ice Age Refrigerator" bought a used refrigerator, advertised as four years old, through an ad in the paper; however, when the icebox failed after only a few days, the plaintiff discovered it was really sixteen years old. The plaintiff filed suit against the seller to recover the $105 she'd paid for the permanently defrosted appliance.

The plaintiff produced a letter from the maker stating that the refrigerator in question had been manufactured in 1965. She also brought along a witness who testified to hearing the defendant tell the plaintiff the fridge was four years young.

Judge Wapner felt the plaintiff had been a little naïve believing she could get a four-year-old refrigerator for $105, but nonetheless he held that the defendant had expressly guaranteed the appliance's age. Normally, a judge would have awarded the difference in value between what the buyer paid for the refrigerator and its actual value. In this case, however, Judge Wapner felt that a sixteen-year-old refrigerator was of such little value that he rescinded the deal. The defendant had to take back her elderly cooler and refund the plaintiff's money.

It's worth noting that the plaintiff in this case was wise to bring along a witness, since she had neither a written warranty nor the ad stating the refrigerator's age. Had the defendant denied the guarantee, and had the plaintiff failed to produce proof, it would have been the plaintiff's word against the defendant's. Since the burden of proof rested on the plaintiff, she might well have lost the case.

In virtually every state there are consumer laws that automatically give buyers a certain type of warranty, called a warranty of merchantability. This warranty, which is implied in most retail sales contracts, but not private party sales, assures that a product is fit for ordinary purposes. If you buy a broom, for instance, it must be fit to sweep a floor without falling to pieces. It doesn't have to be a state-of-the-art broom (whatever that is), but it can't be so ineffective that it belongs in the garbage with the dirt it's supposed to collect. In other words, it must be of average quality.

Thus, if you buy a 1976 Pinto from a car dealer, it doesn't have to purr like a new car, but it must be comparable to the average 1976 Pinto on the market.

The warranty of merchantability doesn't help consumers if they're the cause of the problems with a product. This was the defendant's contention in the case of "The Brainless Computer."

The plaintiffs in this case, a married couple, claimed that the software they'd purchased from the defendant was defective, and they were suing to recover the cost, $1,367. They said the software (and software is the brain of a computer) never functioned, even after the defendant sent someone out to work on it five times.

The defendant's story was a bit different. He said the plaintiffs had purchased a system that allowed them to create their own computer programs, a complicated task that he'd doubted they were up to from the beginning. The defendant told Judge Wapner that after the plaintiffs' failures, he'd had a whiz kid from his staff try to do the programming for them. Unfortunately, his programmer turned out to be less than a wizard and was unable to get the mechanical brain to do any thinking. Finally, however, he sent out a programmer who *did* get everything in order, he said.

Where was this champion programmer? "He couldn't make it today," said the defendant. In computerese, the programmer could have offered a "bit" of data that might have helped the defendant's case.

The defendant also claimed that the wife/plaintiff had told his salesman that the husband/plaintiff had "messed with [the program] and that it was no longer functioning." Where was the salesman? Again, not in court.

The wife denied that the problem with the computer was her husband's fault. Furthermore, she said she'd never told anyone that her husband had "messed" with it. She also submitted "physical evidence" that the program still wasn't working: a blank printout that her computer had produced instead of an inventory list. "It never worked and they were never able to get it to work," she maintained firmly.

Under the warranty of merchantability, said Judge Wapner, the plaintiffs were entitled to software that would be able to create programs, and the evidence that it didn't was strong. The defendant was unable to produce witnesses or other evidence that the problem was the plaintiff's fault or that the problem had been corrected. Therefore, judgment for the plaintiffs in the amount of $1,367.

The warranty of merchantability, like most other laws, is not without exceptions. Under the laws of most states, sellers can limit and even disavow warranties, both explicit warranties and implied warranties of merchantability—but only under certain conditions. If the seller makes it apparent that buyers are purchasing merchandise at their own peril, then they might be out of luck if their products poop out. For instance, if the words "as is" or "with all faults" appear prominently on a sales contract, then let the buyer beware. The buyer who accepts such a contract may have no right to undo the deal or sue for damages. He would only have a case if he could prove that there was fraud in the deal, and fraud is often difficult to prove.

Sometimes a seller will give an explicit warranty but include a clause limiting the damage the customer can collect if the product doesn't live up to the warranty. This was what happened in the case of "The Tire That Went Ka-boom."

The plaintiff in this case claimed that the brand-new radial she'd purchased from the defendant had exploded and blown off her front fender. She was suing for a total of $879: $60 for the busted tire, $536 to repair the fender, $78 for losing a day of work, $25 in towing costs, and $180 for the other three tires she'd bought from the defendant. She was afraid these tires were also defective.

The plaintiff was driving home from work one afternoon, she said, when she heard a loud explosion and felt a sudden rush of air against her face. Now, California motorists are accustomed to things that go bump on the road, but things that go ka-boom can be alarming. Leaping from the driver's seat, she found her new radial a rubbery blob and her front fender mangled. She felt fortunate that she'd been traveling at only ten miles per hour, and she consoled herself that she had a warranty from the defendant.

But the defendant pointed to a prominently displayed clause in the warranty that limited the retailer's damages to the value of the tire. He said he was willing to replace the tire, but that the warranty required him to do no more.

Because the limitation clause was adequately visible, Judge Wapner was bound to enforce it unless he felt it was so unreasonable that it violated some social policy of the state. This wasn't the case here. Therefore, the Judge held that the plaintiff was only entitled to $53, the value of the tire when it blew. He noted, however, that the plaintiff could still sue the manufacturer of the tire, who might be liable for some of the other damages.

The lesson here is that you could blow your case if you don't read your warranty carefully and know just what kind of protection it offers you. If you don't like it, shop around for a better deal.

INSPECTIONS

Under the laws of most states, buyers normally aren't required to inspect a product before they purchase it. If you buy a lawn mower, for instance, you aren't required to give it a going-over in the store. If you find it defective when you get it home, you ordinarily wouldn't lose your right to enforce any warranties it carries just because you decided not to inspect. This applies even if an inspection would have revealed the defect.

There is, however, one major exception. If there was an obvious problem—for instance, if the blade of the mower was falling off and it was apparent to the naked eye when you bought it—then you might compromise your rights by going through with the purchase. The rationale behind this rule is that a buyer who purchases a product in spite of obvious problems knows he's taking a chance.

Legal problems usually arise as a result of halfhearted inspections. Under the laws of most states, when someone undertakes an inspection, he's considered on notice of not only whatever defects are found, but also whatever defects should have been found. Thus, if you ask your mechanic to check out a prospective vehicle and he performs an inspection that's more like a dusting than a spring housecleaning, you could be in trouble.

SHODDY GOODS

Remember, when the buyer inspects, the law deems him or her *on notice as to any defects that a reasonable inspection would uncover.* Thus, in a way, a cursory inspection is really worse than no inspection at all.

The plaintiff in the case of "The Red-hot Capri" paid $1,250 for a ten-year-old Capri, only to have it backfire and catch fire on the freeway. The car was burned beyond repair, and the plaintiff was pretty burned up too. She said the defendant—a private party—had told her the car "did backfire, but there was nothing to worry about." She test-drove it and it backfired, but she decided to buy it anyhow.

The defendant denied ever telling the plaintiff there was nothing to worry about. She claimed she'd told the plaintiff that the car backfired sometimes, but not often, and that the carburetor needed cleaning. She felt the plaintiff had known what she was buying.

Noting that there was no warranty here, only ordinary seller's puffery, Judge Wapner ruled that the plaintiff had been on notice about the backfiring problem. (The warranty of merchantability only applies to retail sales, not private party sales.) The defendant had told her about it, and her test drive constituted an inspection of sorts. "You purchased a ten-year-old car with a broken odometer, so you had no way of knowing how many miles were on it," Judge Wapner reminded the plaintiff. He felt she shouldn't have limited her inspection to a simple test drive. Thus, the plaintiff's case backfired too; judgment for the defendant.

BUYER ABUSE

Although state legislatures during the last fifteen years have voted aye on a slew of consumer protection laws, they haven't been insensitive to the rights of sellers. For instance, some legislatures have passed laws ordering judges to look closely at defective-products cases in which the buyer has used the product. After all, there's always the possibility that the buyer is responsible for the problems with the product.

"The Bald Tires" involved a tire seller who pinned the blame for a blowout on the buyer instead of the tire. He said the plaintiff's tire had gone bust because it was worn out as a result of improper alignment, not because of any inherent defect.

"Our warranty covers the manufacturer's workmanship and material," explained the defendant. "If there is improper inflation or misalignment, then the warranty becomes null and void."

The defendant went on to say that when a tire he sold became unserviceable, he ordinarily assigned it a value based on how much tread was left. Then he gave the customer an allowance for that amount on a new tire. In this case, he'd offered to replace the plaintiff's tire for $25—a $10 savings over the regular price.

The plaintiff had refused, however, insisting on a full refund of the $35 he'd paid fo the tire. He contended that his wheels were perfectly in line and, what was more, that the defendant's shop had performed the alignment one month after he purchased the tire.

"Where's the receipt?" challenged the defendant.

"I don't have one," said the plaintiff.

Judge Wapner felt the fact that the plaintiff had neglected the tire until it blew indicated he wasn't taking good care of his car. Furthermore, the plaintiff couldn't prove his wheels were aligned. "You should have taken [the defendant's] offer for a new tire," the Judge told the plaintiff. Judgment for the defendant.

Sellers might also find protection under the law from customers who have unreasonable expectations of what a product should do. The plaintiff in the case of "The Shoes That

Sprung a Leak,'' for example, believed the pair of shoes he'd bought from the defendant should have been waterproof; the defendant felt this was not only unreasonable, but ridiculous.

The plaintiff was suing for a $40 refund on a pair of shoes that had become waterlogged when he wore them during a rainstorm. He believed that shoes should be able to stand up to the weather as a matter of course. He said that he hadn't worn rubbers once in the thirty years he'd lived in sunny California, come rain or come shine, and his feet had never taken a soaking. Had the defendant warned him that these shoes required galoshes, he never would have bought them, he said.

His wife supported this assertion. Her husband would never wear galoshes, she said.

Granted Southern California has a dry climate and Southern Californians—especially motorists—are notoriously inept at dealing with the rain; even so, Judge Wapner felt it wasn't quite fair to expect leather to rise above the laws of nature. Into each life a little rain must fall, and into each shoe a little puddle will seep. The defendant would just have to get over his dislike of galoshes. Judge Wapner held for the defendant, and, as it was a rainy day, he graciously gave the plaintiff his pair of rubbers to wear. The plaintiff didn't leave the court singing in the rain, but let's hope he arrived home with dry feet.

FRAUD

Regardless of warranties and regardless of limitations on warranties, courts will generally allow buyers to get out of deals if they can prove they were defrauded. If the buyer can prove that a seller's fraudulent statement was a material part of the deal—that is, if he can prove that it was a primary reason for the buyer's choosing to make the purchase—then the judge can rescind it. This means the seller will get back the product and the buyer will get back the purchase price. In addition, the buyer could be entitled to punitive damages, which serve as punishment for intentional misconduct.

Proving fraud can be a problem. How do you prove that the seller was stating something about the product that he knew wasn't true? How do you prove the seller deliberately withheld information about a product's defects?

Supporting allegations like these isn't impossible but it can be difficult. The plaintiff in the case of "The Cracked Sapphire," for example, was alleging that the defendant, a jeweler, had purposely tried to substitute a flawed ring for the perfect one she paid for. However, she learned that proving fraud can be as hard as a diamond.

First of all, the plaintiff explained that she'd only chosen the ring in the first place because of the "clear blue sapphire" at its center. In legal terms, this meant that the excellent condition of the stone was a material part of the deal. After giving the defendant a check for $292, she'd left the ring with him to be sized. When she returned to pick it up, she said, she noticed a white speck on the sapphire, which led her to believe the defendant had switched stones on her. She refused to take possession of the ring and filed a suit to recover the purchase price.

The defendant showed Judge Wapner two rings: the one he said the plaintiff had purchased and then refused to accept after sizing, and one he said he'd later offered her just to keep the peace. The Judge examined the two rings and saw no imperfections in either. He asked the plaintiff to point out the stone with the imperfection.

"Neither of these is the one I'm talking about," she said after examining them.

The defendant explained that he'd never claimed the stone

was perfect; indeed, perfect sapphires command much higher prices. He admitted there was a very slight imperfection in one of the stones, but said the imperfection was visible only with a loupe and had been there when the plaintiff picked out the ring originally.

The plaintiff, however, still insisted that she'd seen the flaw with her naked eye, and that neither ring the defendant had brought to court was the one he'd tried to give her.

Judge Wapner suggested the plaintiff take the ring the jeweler had offered as a replacement. She could either do that or abide by his judgment, he said.

But the plaintiff was adamant: "I just want a refund because I don't want to do business with him," she said.

In his decision, Judge Wapner explained that he encouraged settlements at all times. He ruled that there was no evidence that the ring had been switched other than the plaintiff's *unsupported* contention. He noted that there was no visible flaw in the ring in question and that, furthermore, the defendant was correct in saying that a perfect gem can't be bought for $300.

"I can't refund your money because there is no proof of misrepresentation," explained the Judge. "If the flaw was obvious, you should have seen it when you picked out the ring, because it's not likely it could have been damaged during sizing."

Judge Wapner said that the plaintiff would have to accept the ring with the flaw, unless the defendant was still willing to give her the replacement ring. He was, and the plaintiff was very fortunate. When the judge gives a hint like the one Judge Wapner gave this plaintiff, it's a good idea to take it.

Proving an allegation of fraud requires presenting a very convincing case in court. You don't have to be F. Lee Bailey to win, but you may have to do a lot of footwork to garner ample evidence.

THE PEOPLE'S COURT

The plaintiff in the case of "The Lady and the Tainted Tire" went to admirable lengths in trying to prove that the defendant had sold her a damaged tire by claiming it was new. She said the defendant had told her it was a new tire worth $92 and that he was letting her have it cheap for $41.

She later found out that the tire was blemished, so she went to the police. She presented them with her receipt, which explicitly stated the tire was new. She also offered them a report from another tire dealer confirming that the tire was no good.

The police approached the defendant with the plaintiff's charges, but he denied them. He gave the police a copy of the receipt he said he'd given the plaintiff; this receipt said the tire was blemished.

In court, the defendant submitted yet another copy of the receipt to Judge Wapner; this one didn't state that the tire was either new or blemished.

In presenting her case to Judge Wapner, the plaintiff submitted copies of both the receipt that said the tire was new and the one that said it wasn't. She also presented the affidavit from the other tire dealer and the police report, which concluded that the receipt the defendant produced had been altered.

The three conflicting receipts and the police report convinced the Judge that the plaintiff had been defrauded. He believed the defendant had misrepresented the tire as new, knowing it wasn't.

Commending the plaintiff for a well-presented case, Judge Wapner awarded her $31 for her tire's present value. He also awarded her punitive damages totaling $450.

Thus, the defendant learned a costly lesson about fraud, one that should teach you a valuable lesson about making a purchase. Save your receipts and, if you feel you were cheated, try to compile compelling evidence before going to court. Remember that the burden of proof lies on you.

PRODUCT LIABILITY

In the past, judges wouldn't impose liability on anyone who'd done nothing wrong. A person had to be considered somewhat at fault—through negligence, willful misconduct, or some other means—to be held liable under the law. Manufacturers could get off the legal hook simply by using *reasonable care* in making a product.

Until recently, this blame-oriented method of imposing liability produced harsh result for consumers who purchased defective products. If a manufacturer employed the latest technology and followed the highest available safety standards in producing a product, it was extremely difficult for a consumer who got a lemon, or even one who was injured by the product, to successfully recover damages—from either the manufacturer or the retailer. After all, neither had done anything wrong. They'd done the best they could. The consumer ordinarily could win a lawsuit *only* by proving that the manufacturer had failed to use reasonable care and state-of-the-art technology.

Over the last twenty-five years, this theory has been re-evaluated in many states. Critics argue that the unlucky consumer who happens to get the bad apple out of the bunch shouldn't have to bear the entire loss. They maintain that the consumer has done nothing wrong either and, moreover, gets stuck with defective products merely by chance.

Imposing liability on the manufacturer automatically, without respect to fault, is a better solution, the critics contend. They reason that if the manufacturer is held legally responsible, he'll pass the cost of a judgment on to *all* consumers in the form of higher prices. Thus, all consumers pay a *little* for the mistake, rather than one unlucky consumer paying for all of it.

This theory of imposing automatic liability without regard to fault is called strict liability, and many states have adopted it. When it applies to merchandise, it's also called products liability. As a further advantage to the consumer, many states hold retailers as well as manufacturers strictly liable. Thus, if the manufacturer is located thousands of miles away from an injured consumer, the consumer could elect to sue his local retailer; then the retailer could turn around and sue the manufacturer.

Another rationale behind the strict liability theory is that imposing liability encourages manufacturers to make better, safer products. If they don't, and litigants win a number of judgments against them, the costs they incur will have to be passed on to consumers and will eventually price their products out of the market. Therefore, they have an incentive to exercise more caution and develop better technology.

In the case of "Danger in the Dressing Room," the plaintiff was suing a clothing boutique for injuries she'd received on her thumb while trying on a metal belt. She claimed the belt was defective and was seeking $1,000—a combination of medical expenses, compensation for lost wages, and compensation for pain and suffering.

The defendant, the owner of the boutique, produced the belt in court as evidence. It looked harmless enough, but the plaintiff said that the defendant had folded material over the sharp edges and taped it down. The defendant denied having tampered with the belt; his wife, who'd been the plaintiff's saleslady, said that the material had been folded down in just that way when she'd given the belt to the plaintiff to try on, but that the material had been folded up, exposing the sharp edges, when the plaintiff had returned it.

SHODDY GOODS

The defendant also disputed the plaintiff's injury. The defendant characterized it as a "pinprick," but the plaintiff claimed it had required two stitches. The plaintiff, however, had no proof of treatment.

It was at this point that the case got a bit nasty. The defendant's wife claimed that the plaintiff had come into the store drunk, run around topless, and "took the whole shop apart." She also said the plaintiff had returned three days after the incident with no bandage or mention of a cut.

The plaintiff said she'd returned the next day—with a bandage. As to the allegation regarding her behavior, she said, "That's a lie. . . . I had on my bra and shorts."

In chambers, Judge Wapner did a little investigating via Ma Bell. He phoned the plaintiff's doctor, who corroborated that she'd been given two stitches and a tetanus shot, at a cost of $250; the doctor, however, said that the injury shouldn't have interfered with the plaintiff's work.

Back on the bench, Judge Wapner explained that the retailer is liable for any product defect that existed at the time the product left the manufacturer's control. (The retailer could sue the manufacturer for the amount of the consumer's judgment against the retailer.) He believed that the injury in this case was the result of a design defect in the product, not the plaintiff's carelessness. The judge awarded the plaintiff $250 for medical expenses and $250 for pain and suffering. He made no award for lost wages.

7

SERVICES THAT DO A DISSERVICE

Grooming services
Social services
Business services
Damages for substandard services

When you hire someone to perform a service, you're legally not entitled to expect perfection, much less miracles. If you expect your hairdresser to make you look like Elizabeth Taylor and you end up looking more like Elizabeth the queen, you may be out of luck—legally and otherwise.

The law entitles you to "ordinary care and diligence," meaning the job doesn't have to be the best in the world, but it can't be the worst either. In other words, an evaluation of "mediocre" by others in the same line of work is sufficient to allow a judge to rule for the defendant.

Although this might appear to be a vague and highly subjective yardstick, it's the measure used in most lawsuits in-

SERVICES THAT DO A DISSERVICE

volving allegedly substandard services. A sampling of some cases from *The People's Court* will give you an idea of how "ordinary care and diligence" translates into what you can expect from someone who supplies you with a service.

GROOMING SERVICES

Haven't we all been sorely disappointed by hollow promises of glamour? But who's to blame when promises of beauty fall short of the mark—the stylist or the mirror?

When the subjective world of beauty collides with the courtroom, it can turn into a hair-pulling match. Basically, a consumer's legal rights depend on the type of promise the stylist makes. The following, for example, are forms of puffery that carry no legal weight:

- Trust me, you'll look beautiful.
- You'll look like a different person.
- You'll get nothing but compliments.
- I can do wonders with that hair.
- It can't be any worse than what you have now.

Precision cuts notwithstanding, such promises are simply too imprecise. Vague statements don't constitute legally binding warranties. Most consumers, however, never think to pin the stylist down. For instance, if you give your stylist a picture and tell him or her to match the cut, you could have a case if the finished product differs from the one in the photo. You must realize, however, that to fulfill the promise, the stylist only has to re-create the look of the cut in the photo; you could look like hell, but the stylist, having matched the cut, would still be off the hook. After all, it isn't the stylist's fault if a Morgan Fairchild coif makes you look like Lassie.

Usually, consumers don't get specific guarantees in advance, making their stylists legally responsible only for exercising "ordinary care."

The case of "Hair Today, Gone Tomorrow" was typical of how a beautification plan winds up in a courtroom. This case involved a woman who asked her stylist for a permanent and got permanent damage. The woman claimed the stylist had left the solution on too long and burned her scalp, resulting in hair loss and scarring.

The stylist tried to convince the court that the plaintiff had simply suffered an allergic reaction to the solution—a fluke that the stylist couldn't reasonably have been expected to anticipate. But Judge Wapner wasn't convinced, since the plaintiff was able to prove that an identical solution had been applied to her hair before, with no adverse effects. He awarded the plaintiff not only the cost of the cut, but her medical expenses and compensation for pain and suffering as well.

In another, more bizarre fiasco, the case of "The Scissors-Happy Stylist," the plaintiff claimed she'd been scalped, 1980's style. As she explained to Judge Wapner, "I asked for a trim. He started cutting, and about fifteen minutes into the cut I noticed he was dancing around my head, laughing and acting wildly. I was very upset. I said I didn't like the cut. He just took a razor and shaved the back of my hair line."

The defendant countered that dancing simply wasn't his style. Furthermore, he said, razors were "passé." He used clippers.

The defendant was cut down to size when the plaintiff called her witness, a stylist with nineteen years of experience, who said she'd never seen such a hatchet job. According to the stylist, no man would want to touch the plaintiff —the back of her neck felt like whisker stubble. The witness felt that a hedger or some other deadly weapon—certainly

SERVICES THAT DO A DISSERVICE

*The defendant demonstrates his styling technique
in the case of "The Scissors-Happy Stylist."*

not an innocuous pair of clippers—must have been employed to achieve such total destruction.

After viewing some not-so-pretty pictures, Judge Wapner
was sufficiently convinced to award the plaintiff damages. She
did not, however, recover for any loss of companionship, even
though a woman with whisker stubble might not make for a
very romantic evening.

SOCIAL SERVICES

When parties become the subjects of lawsuits, it's a safe
bet that a good time wasn't had by all.

Take the wedding in the case of "The Bride That Cried."
The plaintiffs planned a formal wedding to end all weddings,
and they had the pictures of the final event to prove it. The

splendor of the bridal gown was matched only by the bride herself. The groom was dashingly bedecked in a tux, and there were flowers, flowers everywhere, arranged to perfection. Things couldn't have been better—except for the disc jockey.

According to the bride and groom, the disc jockey arrived just minutes before the ceremony, looking as if he'd just rolled out of bed. He appeared in a T-shirt, jeans, and a curious type of "natural" hair style. The plaintiffs also contended that the bride had had to make her dramatic entrance down the winding staircase to the accompaniment of nothing but her own astonishment. By the time she began her walk down the aisle, astonishment had turned to anger. It was the one time in her life she'd wanted to face the music, and there was nothing but conspicuous silence.

It wasn't until she began her final approach to the altar, she said, that the music finally chimed in. Unfortunately, instead of playing the "Wedding March" ("Here comes the bride, da, *da,* da, da . . ."), the D.J. played the exit music.

And this wasn't the only time he had the bride marching to a different drummer. While the minister was explaining the meaning of life, death, and eternity, the D.J. simply couldn't forever hold his peace, it seemed. He chose this inopportune moment to treat the crowd to the pop hit "Whip It."

The D.J. admitted showing up "a few minutes late," but held that he'd arrived at least an hour before vow time. He argued that the bride hadn't given him sufficient time to prepare for the ceremony, claiming that he'd received her list of songs only a few days before the event.

As Judge Wapner explained, however, when someone agrees to perform a service, he or she is required to use "ordinary skill and diligence." Had the D.J. said he was unable to perform adequately under the circumstances and the bride still agreed to hire him, maybe the last laugh, or cry, would have been on the bride. But the D.J. had never offered such a warning and was, therefore, on the hook.

The most difficult aspect of this case was determining the damages the newlyweds had suffered. They were suing for the entire cost of the wedding, as well as the groom's medical bills. Yes, the groom had literally been sick over the whole incident and had a videotape of the wedding to prove it. The tape clearly showed considerable stress on the groom's face, especially during the vows, when the bride appeared to be uttering a string of veiled profanities in the groom's direction. Then he fainted in the middle of the ceremony and had to be revived before he could promise to love and honor.

The bride spent her wedding night at her groom's side, but it wasn't exactly the kind of romantic evening she might have planned. It was at his hospital bedside. A wedding night to remember—courtesy, she claimed, of the wayward disc jockey.

Judge Wapner, however, wasn't convinced that the groom's lapse of consciousness was a direct result of the D.J.'s substandard performance. Judge Wapner has performed hundreds of wedding ceremonies over the last twenty years, and has seen the calm couple, the basket cases, and everything in between. He has observed how people react to the pressure of getting hitched. Some drink; some take a pill; some faint.

The plaintiffs had to prove that the fainting spell had been a direct result of the disharmony caused by the music. The doctor's report gave no such indication. Therefore, the plaintiffs' contention was speculative, and they didn't recover their medical expenses.

As for recovering the entire cost of the wedding, the plaintiffs may have damaged their case by submitting pictures of the reception. It appeared that everyone, including the bride and groom, was having a fine time. In short, the D.J. didn't do his job, and for that the plaintiffs recovered the $235 they'd paid him. But Judge Wapner explained that it was unreasonable to charge the disc jockey for the cost of their wedding, and it was speculative that the D.J. had caused the groom to faint.

A Dear Abby—type footnote: Take solace, newlyweds. This bittersweet episode in your life may be upsetting now, but think thirty years down the road. How many people can show their grandchildren a videotape of Grandma uttering vulgarisms underneath her veil and Grandpa fainting at the altar?

Other, less ceremonial cases have found their way through the double doors of *The People's Court.* For instance, in the case of "Unfulfilled Fantasies," the defendant was disappointed with a stripper she'd hired for her boyfriend's birthday party. The defendant didn't think the stripper had gotten down to basics, so she refused to pay the $100 stripping fee.

The defendant charged that the stripper, who was an employee of the Tush-a-Gram Company, hadn't stripped down to a G-string as promised. Instead, she'd worn a bikini bottom. Big deal, the defendant argued, you can go to the beach and see bikini bottoms without paying a cent.

The defendant also complained that the stripper hadn't mingled with the guests.

Judge Wapner asked the defendant if her boyfriend had enjoyed the stripper's act; she replied, "He said he's seen better." This suggested that the boyfriend might not have been as disappointed by the stripper's performance as his girlfriend would have had the court believe. Judge Wapner decided it might be best to have the birthday boy critique the stripper's performance, but the defendant explained that her beau was in another court. Not to worry, though; he was a lawyer. Unfortunately for the defendant, Judge Wapner considered the boyfriend's testimony crucial.

Her star witness in absentia, the defendant knew she was in trouble. In desperation, she explained the bottom line to the Judge: "My boyfriend would have liked the G-string better—wouldn't you?"

Judge Wapner made it clear that he couldn't testify in his own courtroom: "Let's not get into that," he said.

Judge Wapner then turned the case in a more concrete direction by asking the defendant if she had pictures of the party. She happily produced some, thinking they would settle the dispute once and for all. Indeed, they did.

After perusing the photos in chambers, Judge Wapner concluded, "The pictures show me that the stripper was sitting on your boyfriend's lap. No doubt in my mind . . . he was all smiles; he was having a very good time. Furthermore, the stripper was exposed from the waist up. And it's hard to know how she could have 'mingled' much more. True, she didn't wear a G-string, but I think the plaintiff earned her money. Judgment for plaintiff for one hundred dollars."

This case provides an interesting illustration of how someone can win a lawsuit without saying a word. But then, to a stripper, a picture's worth a thousand words.

And the beat goes on. Take the case of "Looking for Love in All the Wrong Places." The defendant paid a dating service $85 in return for a good time. Actually, he was promised more than just a good time. According to the plaintiff, he was promised a girlfriend within two weeks of the date he signed the agreement. But he didn't get a girlfriend. In fact, he didn't even get a decent date. So he sued for a refund.

Being one of the few happily married men of our times, Judge Wapner might have lent a sympathetic ear to the plaintiff's motive for hiring the dating service: "I had experimented with a number of discos and the like, but, frankly, I'm about as popular with women as a porcupine is in a balloon factory. I needed help."

The plaintiff produced a contract that both he and the defendant had signed. He pointed to a clause that guaranteed a full refund if it was still "table for one, please" after two weeks' time.

Burt Reynolds will never know the grief the plaintiff endured. He telephoned the first prospect, but to no avail. She said she didn't like the way he talked, and hung up on him.

He did slightly better the second date around. In fact, he spoke with her by telephone five times. Each time she said she couldn't meet him. Finally, he decided a platonic relationship would be unsatisfactory, much less a telephonic one.

The third strike was the capper. This prospective girlfriend said she would meet with the plaintiff at the stroke of midnight at a gas station in less than romantic East Los Angeles. As the plaintiff explained to Judge Wapner, "I might be from Hialeah but I'm not that dumb."

The defendant protested. First, she countered that the third prospect had agreed to meet the plaintiff in a Denny's Restaurant parking lot, not a gas station. She complained that she'd known the plaintiff was going to be a handful from the beginning. "After talking with him for a few seconds," she said, "I knew it would be difficult to introduce him. . . . He was so nervous."

The defandant should have trusted her instincts and not promised a service she wasn't sure she could deliver. Had she not guaranteed the results, she might have fulfilled her dating-service duty just by providing the plaintiff with an opportunity for meeting women. But she'd rushed in where even Cupid might not have dared to tread. As a result, Judge Wapner awarded the plaintiff his $85 back. The Judge also expressed his hope that the lonely litigant could "shed his porcupine image."

BUSINESS SERVICES

The People's Court has played host to a wide spectrum of business disputes. There was the travel agent who tried to use the 1981 air-traffic controllers' strike as an excuse for failing to deliver a promised vacation package. And there was the debtor who tried to satisfy a $35 loan by cooking dinner for the creditor. Both of these defendants lost their cases, but helped to show the American public that consumers won't accept shoddy business practices sitting down.

The case of "The Battling Babysitter" presented a rip-off that many parents have faced—a negligent babysitter. The plaintiff hired a teenage babysitter to play surrogate mother from nine to five, at a fee of $1.75 per hour, which the defendant felt was top dollar. Therefore, she expected a premium job.

The mother decided that the sitter had done more sitting than babysitting, and she refused to pay. According to the mother, the plaintiff had allowed her boyfriend to "visit" all day. The young girl countered that her beau had sat alone in the den watching television and hadn't interfered with her duties.

The mother also contended that the young woman hadn't followed instructions to water the front lawn and wash the dishes. The babysitter vigorously challenged the mother on both claims, claiming that she'd soaked the lawn and was soaking the last few dishes when the mother returned from work.

The mother was able to supply two important witnesses, her four-year-old son and six-year-old daughter. Both children, who could barely see over the defendant's table, testified that the sitter hadn't watered the lawn and rushed to do some dishes only minutes before their mother returned

143

home. The kids also accused the plaintiff of sleeping on the job during much of the morning.

A more serious allegation surfaced as the case progressed. The mother accused the sitter of leaving the children locked in the house while she made a cigarette run to a nearby liquor store. The plaintiff admitted to going for cigarettes, but said she'd been gone only for ten minutes or so.

The mother's closing salvo was inspirational. "The plaintiff expects me to pay top dollar while all she did was neglect the children and even compromise their safety," she said. It wasn't because of the money that she was refusing to pay, she continued, but to teach this sitter, and perhaps others, that single parents wouldn't stand for such unconscionable treatment.

Judge Wapner didn't have to sit long on the evidence before reaching a verdict. Having weighed the testimony of the children and considered that the babysitter had allowed her boyfriend to visit and had even left the children alone, he concluded, "If the plaintiff expects me to believe she spent most of the day with the children . . . I don't."

Perhaps the plaintiff's credibility was damaged by her cigarette purchase: She was only fifteen years old, and the legal age for buying cigarettes in California is eighteen.

Judge Wapner was especially concerned that the children had been left unattended. What if a fire had broken out while the sitter was gone, he asked, with the children locked helplessly inside the house? The plaintiff was speechless, perhaps horrified at the prospect of what her negligence might have caused.

The Judge, however, was far from speechless. "This could be the subject of a Sunday sermon," he said. He ruled that the plaintiff had supplied a substandard service and had violated her duty to exercise ordinary care and diligence. Congratulating the plaintiff for taking a stand, he explained to the audience that small-claims court is designed for people like this plaintiff—people who have modest disputes that don't justify a lawyer's expertise or bill. In small-claims court, even a recalcitrant babysitter is not beneath—or above—the law.

Another domestic case also serves as a lesson to those who would like to succeed in business without really trying, and to those who would like to stop them. In the case of "The Missing Mother's Helper," the defendants hired a service to find them a housekeeper. The written agreement provided that the defendants would pay the plaintiff a $200 fee when he found an "acceptable" housekeeper.

Although the plaintiff found the defendants an attractive Danish servant, something was rotten in Denmark. First of all, the Nordic bombshell smoked like a chimney, even though the defendants maintained they'd specifically requested a nonsmoker. The defendants decided to let the Dane play house anyhow, but she was hardly there long enough to find the kitchen. She left the first weekend and never returned. Consequently, the defendants refused to pay the plaintiff's fee.

The plaintiff admitted that the defendants had mentioned "something about smoking," but pointed out that this restriction hadn't been incorporated into the agreement. The contract stipulated only an "acceptable" housekeeper. Further, the plaintiff claimed that the housekeeper had been working for the defendants for two weeks before they called to announce the alleged disappearance. As far as the plaintiff was concerned, he'd promised to deliver an acceptable housekeeper and had done just that.

In this "maid-for-TV" lawsuit, the plaintiff learned a few basic legal principles of business. First, the contract that he'd drafted needed a lot of cleaning up, and not by a housekeeper. It was incomprehensible in spots. The law in most states provides that ambiguities in a contract shouldn't be interpreted to the advantage of the person who drafted it. After

all, the writer of a contract is in a position to create or eliminate ambiguities as he sees fit, and the legal system doesn't
want people purposely writing confusing contracts for their
own benefit. Thus, Judge Wapner was bound to interpret
"acceptable" more from the defendants' point of view than
the plaintiff's.

Obviously, only a nonsmoking housekeeper would have
been acceptable to the defendants. Furthermore, any acceptable housekeeper would have worked longer than a week.
Judge Wapner decided that the maid delivered by the plaintiff just wasn't acceptable enough to warrant a finder's fee.

Judge Wapner also noted that the plaintiff was doing business without a license, in direct violation of California law.
For this reason, the Judge explained, even if the plaintiff had
proved his entitlement to a finder's fee under the contract,
he still would have lost the case, since he was doing business illegally.

Sometimes, the finished product isn't the only issue in a
case involving substandard services. In the case of "Take This
Letter and Stuff It," two stockbrokers hired a woman to stuff
envelopes at $6 per hour. The job was simple enough: Fold
three sheets of paper, insert them in a business-size envelope, and repeat two thousand times.

The stuffer said that the task had required thirty-six hours
to complete. Certainly if envelope stuffing were an Olympic
event, thirty-six hours for two thousand wouldn't win a gold
medal.

The stockbrokers paid the woman her due. Shortly thereafter, however, it dawned on them that perhaps the time the
woman had said was involved was excessive. The brokers
decided they'd been ripped off, and they brought their case
to The People's Court for a refund.

The defendant said she'd hired a friend as a sort of sub-
contractor to aid her in the stuffing. She said that she'd spent

eighteen hours on the job and so had her friend—adding up to a total of thirty-six hours of work.

The plaintiffs argued that they'd hired the defendant alone to perform the task, and that if she'd received a little help from her friend—well, that was her business. The plaintiffs held that they were obliged to pay only the defendant for her work.

After lengthy and confusing testimony, it appeared that the defendant hadn't acted improperly by hiring a letter-licking underling. If both women performed their jobs adequately, it could be assumed that it would have taken one person thirty-six hours to perform the task. The bill would have been the same.

But the plaintiffs vigorously challenged the assumption that the two women had done an adequate job. One plaintiff offered evidence that he'd hired a seven-year-old girl to lick a comparable number of envelopes, and she'd finished in less than half the time.

Judge Wapner quizzed the defendant and her assistant about their work habits. They said they'd been efficient and honest in their work. No chitchat, just a lot of stuffing and licking.

Courtroom observers were troubled by this case. How could the Judge resolve it? Even if the plaintiffs had licked at a snail's pace, if they'd performed to the best of their abilities, maybe they should be entitled to keep their fee.

However, Judge Wapner proved to the satisfaction of all doubters that very little could stand in the way of truth and justice. While in chambers, the Judge folded the same packet of materials the defendant had folded, stuffed the materials into the same envelope, and licked it shut. For the sake of accuracy, he repeated the experiment three times.

When explaining the results of his experiment to the court, the Judge pointed out that he'd performed the task at a leisurely pace. Still, by multiplying the number of seconds he'd taken by the number of envelopes the defendant had had to stuff, he calculated that she should have been able to complete the task in half the time.

The defendant and her companion had a legal obligation to perform their task with ordinary skill and diligence. The Judge's experiment and the plaintiffs' testimony made it apparent that the plaintiffs had paid an exorbitant bill. Stopping short of ruling that the defendant had defrauded the plaintiffs, he concluded that the job should have been completed in half the time, and awarded the plaintiffs accordingly. Perhaps the next time the defendant gets a job stuffing envelopes, she'll invest in a damp sponge.

DAMAGES FOR SUBSTANDARD SERVICES

According to a legal theory called substantial performance, if someone undertakes to perform a service but doesn't quite cut the mustard, he or she may still be entitled to a partial fee. Substantial performance allows that employees who perform the bulk of their work satisfactorily are entitled to the agreed-upon fee, less the amount it will cost to complete the job according to specifications.

For example, suppose you hired a contractor to build an addition to your house at a cost of $10,000, and the contractor performed to specifications with one exception: The wiring in one electrical panel was off slightly. Let's say it cost you $400 to correct the wiring problem. Since the contractor performed almost the entire job satisfactorily, he would be entitled to his fee, less the cost of correcting the faulty wiring. In other words, he would still be entitled to $9,600.

In cases in which a laborer attempts to perform a service and succeeds only in small part, however, the customer generally doesn't have to pay anything. If, that is, he or she can prove that the job was so substandard as to be essentially worthless.

In cases in which a laborer does more harm than good (haven't we all met this guy?) he can actually end up owing you money. If, for instance, the contractor above who added the room to your house accidentally started a fire that resulted in $15,000 worth of damage, he could end up owing you $5,000, even if the room addition was eventually completed to specifications.

The bottom line is simple and instructive: Who needs a lawsuit anyway? Shop around before hiring someone. Demand references. Whenever possible, check out the prospective employee's work product, and make sure the contractor is licensed.

Above all, *never rely on a handshake,* or, for that matter, a kiss. Commit the agreement to *writing.* If the stakes are high, make sure a lawyer reviews the agreement before you sign it. Otherwise, we'll see you in court.

8

A LOAN AGAIN

No love lost over loans
Investment loans
Friendship loans

Many *People's Court* litigants have unwittingly parodied Greta Garbo: "But I wanted it to be a loan," they've said.

This is a chapter devoted to good intentions gone awry. Have you ever loaned money to a friend, only to have him insist later that it was a gift, not a loan? Or maybe he said that he'd already repaid you, sure, you remember. Or, worse yet, maybe he denied the loan entirely—"Loan? What loan?"

Any lawyer worth his three-piece suit will tell you to get everything in writing—and to dot all the *i*'s and cross all the *t*'s. But what do lawyers know about personal relationships? If they understood people so well, they wouldn't always rate a notch above used-car salesmen in polls measuring public esteem.

A LOAN AGAIN

True, it's tough to deal with friends in a businesslike manner. It seems outrageous to ask a friend to sign a promissory note. After all, everyone knows that such notes are only needed to document a loan in the event of a lawsuit. And how dare you even consider suing your neighbor, your friend, or your lover!

The fact is, *The People's Court* at times looks like *The Dating Game* gone wrong. A steady stream of litigants have been embarrassed to tell Judge Wapner that they didn't think to put the loan in writing because they trusted the debtor. But when the debtor begins dating your boyfriend or girlfriend, trust evaporates and tempers flare. Sometimes honesty falls by the wayside as well.

Even though you shouldn't *appear* distrustful, it's not a bad idea to *be* a bit distrustful when loaning out your hard-earned cash. When making a loan, there are ways to protect yourself without appearing offensive or suspicious. For instance, when you make the loan, have several witnesses present. They can help you establish the creation of the loan, the amount, and the terms of repayment. The witnesses should be as neutral as possible. They shouldn't be relatives. Friends are okay, but make sure they're trusted friends who will come to your aid if you need them.

Another precaution you can take is to always loan money in the form of a check. At the bottom of the check, on the memo line, write the word "loan." Of course, this method isn't foolproof. You could, after all, write in "loan" after the check cleared. But if it's done with the same pen as the other information, you could have a strong case—especially if witnesses were present.

You should also establish a time for repayment. Vague statements like "I'll pay you as soon as I get the money" or "Don't worry, I'll pay you soon" can only lead to trouble and sore feelings. You may feel embarrassed about asking for a repayment schedule, but so be it. After all, you're doing a favor, and if your friend is offended by such a reasonable request, then maybe you should think twice before making the loan. Just ask yourself, "What would Ann Landers do?"

Under the laws of most states, if you can establish that you loaned someone money, the debtor has the burden of proving in court that the loan was repaid. In other words, going into court, it's assumed that you haven't been repaid. If the debtor can't prove repayment, you could win the case. This is why it's very important that you be able to establish that you made the loan. This is also why you should never loan cash, unless you have a specific written agreement verifying the loan.

NO LOVE LOST OVER LOANS

The most common loan disputes in *The People's Court* seem to involve dissolved love relationships. One thing has become clear to *People's Court* viewers: In love, neither a borrower nor a lender be.

The case of "The Merry Christmas Loan" serves as a good reminder that love and money don't mix. According to the plaintiff, he'd loaned the defendant, an attractive young lady, $500 to visit her family in Arizona for Christmas. He said the defendant had told him she worked for a well-known jewelry store and promised she would be able to pay him back after collecting her commissions for the Christmas season.

The plaintiff also said that the green-eyed monster jealousy was standing between him and his greenbacks. He alleged that the defendant was refusing to pay out of anger because he'd taken a younger lady to Mexico on a cruise. Judge Wapner didn't pursue the details of this fiesta, but the plaintiff unwittingly provided some insight into his character nonetheless when he said, "I don't give that kind of money

A LOAN AGAIN

*The litigants in the case of
"The Merry Christmas Loan."*

to women I don't sleep with." He then showed the Judge a canceled check for $500 made out to the defendant and bearing the word "loan."

The defendant had a somewhat different tale to tell. She said she'd dined several times with the plaintiff and that he'd often made the rather ungentlemanly observation "When you're with me, it doesn't cost you anything." When she finally decided that maybe he wasn't the kind of guy she wanted to see after all, she said, he began harassing her and telling people he was going to sic the Mafia on her.

The defendant acknowledged that the plaintiff had given her the check, but said that he'd told her, "Don't worry about it . . . no problem." She denied that the check had had the word "loan" written on it at the time he gave it to her. The defendant also alleged that the plaintiff, a man much older than she, was what's commonly known as a dirty old man.

Choosing to ignore the more salacious aspects of this case, Judge Wapner got right to the part that wasn't X rated. He felt that the check provided conclusive evidence that the defendant had received the money, so the burden of proving that the check was a gift instead of a loan rested on the defendant. Since she was unable to prove that it was more likely than not that the money was a gift, the Judge ruled for the plaintiff.

In another love-related loan, the plaintiff had a canceled check marked "loan," but the defendant had a photocopy of the same check that was conspicuously missing the important word.

The plaintiff in this one claimed he'd loaned his pretty young neighbor $100 to help her move. The defendant, however, said she'd been told to consider the $100 an early birthday gift. According to her, it was only after she rebuffed his advances that the money became a loan.

The plaintiff denied any attraction to the defendant. He described their relationship as "just friends." They'd never shared more than a spaghetti dinner at his place, he said. Like the plaintiff above, he produced a check made out to the defendant with the word "loan" written on it.

The defendant insisted, however, that the money had been a gift. She said that the plaintiff had offered to "give [her] an extra hundred bucks" when she'd complained to him about money. At first, she said, she refused his offer because she was out of work and didn't know when she would be able to pay him back. But when she expressed her concern, he told her, "That's all right. I can afford it. I have a good-paying job. Just consider this an early birthday gift."

The defendant went on to say that after the gift, the plaintiff had kept after her to come up and see him some time. But apparently she was fed up with spaghetti and/or the plaintiff.

A LOAN AGAIN

The defendant produced a photocopy of the same check the defendant had entered as evidence, only hers conspicuously didn't have the word "loan" on it.

During the commercial break, the audience wondered who was telling the truth. The plaintiff could have written "loan" on the check after getting it back from the bank, but, on the other hand, the defendant could have done some clever photocopying.

Fortunately, the plaintiff admitted that he'd written "loan" on the check's memo line after he got it back from the bank, but only because he'd forgotten to do so when writing the check. And what difference did it make *when* he'd written the word? A loan is a loan is a loan.

It made plenty of difference to Judge Wapner. He ruled that, since the check had been marked "loan" after the fact, and since there was compelling evidence that the plaintiff was a scorned lover, the money must have been a gift. A gift is irrevocable, meaning the giver can't turn it into a loan just because he gets miffed. Therefore, the Judge found for the defendant.

As to why the defendant had possessed the foresight to photocopy the check, we'll never know. Lover's intuition?

Cases involving prenuptial agreements might sometimes seem like loan cases, but they fall under the jurisdiction of divorce judges, not small-claims-court judges. These agreements, which are currently popular with celebrities and others who want to protect both the assets they bring into a marriage and future earnings, establish the property rights of a man and a woman when they marry. "Promises, Promises" was a case involving a prenuptial agreement that mistakenly landed in *The People's Court*.

The plaintiff in this case, the wife, claimed she'd paid for her wedding with the understanding that her husband, the defendant, would pay two months' rent on their apartment and all their telephone bills, in return. The defendant, however, said he'd never made such a deal. He held that it's merely traditional for the bride or her family to pay for the wedding, and who was he to break with tradition, even if the family was breaking up?

Judge Wapner said that since the couple was seeking a divorce, a divorce judge, not he, would have to try the case. Small-claims-court judges don't have the jurisdiction to settle property rights in a divorce, he explained.

But the Judge did issue a warning that anyone considering a prenuptial agreement should heed: This is a special class of agreement that must be in writing to be enforceable. In this particular case, since the plaintiff didn't have the agreement in writing, she might run into a big problem in divorce court. So beware, husbands and wives.

INVESTMENT LOANS

You can't get rich from a paycheck. Any financial adviser worth his calculator will tell you that. Even large salaries— the six-figure variety—won't buy a ticket to the elusive Easy Street. However, there are many who believe you can make a lot more by daredevil investing than by tucking spare cash away in a modest money-market account. In fact, some of these "believers" are such pals they'll even help you get rich quick—with your money, of course.

These kindly souls usually have phone numbers that begin with 800, and the really prudent investor never lets his fingers do the walking into the clutches—even if they're giving away free Veg-O-Matics.

Perhaps the most difficult sales pitch to walk away from is the one delivered by a friend or associate who's "going to make millions" on a "surefire" investment. You've probably met this guy before. He says things like:

A LOAN AGAIN

- I've run it by dozens of people and they all say they'd buy it if it were on the market.
- I've got others who are dying to invest.
- If you invest, you'll make a fortune. Guaranteed.

Words like these have caused many an eye to light up with dollar signs. With every opportunity, however, comes a risk. Sure, some succeed, but many more fail. If it were as easy to get rich as these sharpies make it sound, they would be vacationing at their châteaus on the Riviera instead of hassling you.

People who want your money are all too aware of your fear of losing it and have invented a variety of ways to make it seem as if your investment were guaranteed. They can dance around the risk factor as deftly as Ann Miller can tap across a stage. Their most common routine is to make your investment *sound* like a loan when it really isn't.

This was what happened to the plaintiff in the case of "No Love Lost over Weight Loss." This woman believed she'd loaned the defendant $1,500 to help develop a "surefire" weight-loss device called Shed-A-Body. The defendant, however, argued that the money had been an investment, not a loan, and that when the project had fallen apart, so had the plaintiff's investment.

The plaintiff explained that the defendant had given her a razzle-dazzle pitch. He'd consulted with Muhammad Ali and sports guru Angelo Dundee, he told her. He convinced the plaintiff her money would compound quicker than the federal deficit. And, to top it off, the sweet-talker told her that this was "a loan with love."

But, in court at least, the defendant sang a less passionate tune. He claimed he'd warned the plaintiff at least once not to invest because it was "a risky time." Therefore, the plaintiff should have known the money she'd plunked down was an investment, he said, and not a loan. The defendant also told the court he'd been very specific with the plaintiff, making it clear she wouldn't receive anything unless the Shed-A-Body was marketed.

Judge Wapner shed any doubts as to what was the major problem with this case: Neither party had anything in writing. It was almost ludicrous, said the Judge, to try to sort out such loose conversations after the fact. But, based on the defendant's vague promises, the Judge could only conclude that the plaintiff had known she was taking a risk. She hadn't received any binding guarantees. This looked to Judge Wapner like a case of sour grapes, so he ruled for the defendant.

Fat-free investments seem to be popular in *The People's Court*. In another case, "The Invention That Went Bust," the plaintiff claimed that she'd loaned the defendant money to market a new exercise product called Save-A-Body.

The defendant claimed that the plaintiff had known this was a high-risk operation. He said he'd never made grandiose promises, but rather made it clear that this was a chancy investment that could pay off big.

Unlike the plaintiff in the Shed-A-Body case, this one didn't dispute the way the defendant had presented the project, but she vehemently denied ever having considered her money an investment instead of a loan. Unfortunately for her, however, she couldn't produce proof that she was entitled to repayment. To the contrary, she admitted that she'd been aware of the purpose for which the money was to be used. And she admitted expecting profits from any successful marketing, although the profit distribution was unclear.

As Judge Wapner explained, the expectations of profits were a telling factor in this case. He who reaps the rewards also bears the burdens of failure. As far as the Judge was concerned, this case had investment written all over it. Therefore, again, judgment for the defendant.

A LOAN AGAIN

Interestingly, the outcome of both cases might have been different had the plaintiffs memorialized in writing that they were loaning, not investing, their money—if that was indeed what they believed they were doing. Because they didn't put it in writing, and because the circumstances indicated the contrary, they lost.

FRIENDSHIP LOANS

You'd think by now people would be on to the proverbial "friend in need"; but, if *The People's Court* is any indication, friends, like lovers, find it hard to say no when someone they're close to gets in a jam. Unfortunately, also as with lovers, it's not easy asking a friend to sign a written I.O.U. And you never really know a friend's true colors until something goes wrong.

The case of "The Dog Food Loan," for example, concerned a man and woman who weren't involved romantically, but became involved financially when the plaintiff loaned her male friend $35 for dog food. In this case, there was no argument that the $35 had been a loan; the issue was repayment.

The defendant said that he'd taken the plaintiff out to dinner on three occasions, and he felt that this should constitute repayment. The plaintiff, however, maintained indignantly, "I don't need you to take me to dinner. I want my thirty-five dollars back."

The defendant countered that the plaintiff had waived her right to the $35 because "she ate the dinners." Furthermore, the defendant said, they'd enjoyed "a good, friendly time" together. An unusual defense, and unlike any other that Judge Wapner had come across in twenty years on the bench.

Judge Wapner ruled that the loan had to be repaid. Unless it's been agreed to in advance, taking a friend out to dinner doesn't constitute repayment—no matter how good the restaurant.

The plaintiff in the case of "The Welcome Mat That Got Stepped On" claimed that he'd opened his heart and home to a young couple, supplying them with food, money, and his services; however, they'd rather ungratefully refused to repay him $250, the cost of all his kindness.

The plaintiff said he'd loaned the defendants $20 for gas, $100 for groceries, and $10 in cash. The remainder of the $250, he said, was for various miscellaneous expenses. The plaintiff went on to explain how he'd felt sorry for the couple because they were going to have a baby and were in need of money and food. He'd even given them a key to his apartment, so they could use his kitchen; they had no cooking facilities where they lived.

The defendants, however, said they'd been overwhelmed, so to speak, by the plaintiff's goodness. They claimed that he'd volunteered his services and had even forced his generosity on them. They maintained that, except for a $25 loan, there had never been any mention of repayment.

Judge Wapner said that although the plaintiff was "a very nice gentleman, a Good Samaritan," except for the $25 there appeared to be no understanding that the plaintiff's expenditures were to be repaid. Because the plaintiff couldn't meet his burden of proving the rest of the loan existed, he wasn't entitled to collect it.

The case of "The Teenage Big Spender" involved somewhat misguided generosity. The teenage plaintiff in this case withdrew nearly $1,000 from his savings account, all of which he gave to his "friend," the defendant, in the form of cash, merchandise, and entertainment.

The plaintiff claimed that everything he'd done for the defendant was intended as a loan, but the defendant said that repayment had never been mentioned. The defendant fur-

A LOAN AGAIN

The defendants discuss the decision with Doug Llewelyn in the case of "The Teenage Big Spender."

ther explained that the plaintiff had showered him with gifts in an attempt to buy his friendship.

The defendant was able to produce many witnesses to support his assertion. These witnesses maintained that the plaintiff had quite a reputation for "playing the big shot." According to them, the plaintiff had frequently taken the defendant out to dinner and bought him gifts, simply because he liked to ride in the defendant's car and to be in his company.

It later came out that the plaintiff hadn't mentioned the word "loan" until his father had questioned him about the withdrawals from his savings account. Apparently, it was the father who'd pushed the boy to sue his so-called friend.

Naturally, Judge Wapner sympathized with the plaintiff in this sad story. But he had to rule that since the plaintiff could produce no concrete proof that a loan existed, and since there were witnesses who corroborated the defendant's story, the plaintiff wasn't entitled to repayment. This young plaintiff had to learn the hard way that friendship cannot be bought, but can only be given away.

What all of these cases should make clear is the importance of getting your loan in writing. This means creating an I.O.U. that documents the amount of the loan, the terms of repayment, and any interest that's agreed upon. If installments are required, be sure to specify the dates upon which payments are to be made. The note should also give the creditor the option to immediately demand payment in full if the debtor misses a payment.

Inclusion of a repayment date is essential to the interests of both parties. If the loan has no repayment date, many courts will make the debtor pay on demand. However, from the lender's point of view, having a note with a specific repayment date makes it much harder for the debtor to be unreasonable.

If interest is involved in the terms of the loan, be sure that the amount of interest is specified. Most states limit the amount of interest that can be charged on a personal loan, and if this limit is exceeded, it could constitute usury. If a judge ruled that the terms constituted usury, the creditor would still recover the principal, but would probably forfeit any interest. For instance, if the note specified 12 percent interest and the legal limit was 10, a judge probably wouldn't reduce the rate to 10 percent, but would declare the interest clause of the agreement invalid and award no interest at all. So check with a lawyer to ascertain the legal limit in your state. (In California, ordinarily it's 10 percent.)

And remember: Don't worry about offending the debtor by getting a written I.O.U. This will give you peace of mind, and the debtor, whom you're doing a favor, shouldn't want to deny you that. An I.O.U. that contains the information

A LOAN AGAIN

outlined above and is signed by both parties fixes the rights of each and avoids disputes that could arise later as the result of hazy memories. If you think a friendship is too fragile to withstand a request for an I.O.U., wait and see what a date in court can do to it.

9

CONTRACTS: DOTTED-LINE DILEMMAS

**What happens when there isn't a specific
agreement on price?
What if you're pressured into signing a contract?
What are the special rules governing contracts
with minors?
When can you break a contract?**

Rarely does a day pass without Judge Wapner explaining to a *People's Court* litigant that if he'd committed his deal to writing, he could have nipped his legal dispute in the jurisprudential bud.

Laypeople suffer under the misimpression that they can't draft a valid contract without the assistance of a lawyer. Nothing could be further from the truth. Although you may have seen contracts replete with Latin terms and convoluted sentences, looking as if they were drafted in Rome in the year 1080, a valid contract can be drafted in simple English on a

CONTRACTS: DOTTED-LINE DILEMMAS

napkin in a restaurant. It doesn't even have to be written in complete sentences, or, for that matter, written at all.

That's right, an oral contract can be legally binding, although there are some exceptions. Many states, for example, require that contracts for the sale of real estate must be in writing to be enforceable. Even if an oral contract is valid, there might be problems in enforcing it, especially if the other party denies its existence. If there are no witnesses and one party denies the contract exists, an oral agreement may be worth no more than the paper it isn't written on.

Still, unless a contract involves high stakes or seems unduly complicated, it's unnecessary to involve an attorney.

To be considered legally binding, a contract has to meet several basic requirements. First, there must be an offer. A statement such as "I may sell you my car for $1,500" doesn't constitute an offer, because it's too equivocal. It doesn't express a clear intention to sell the car; it only indicates the possibility is being considered. Only a definite statement, such as "I will sell you my car for $1,500," constitutes an offer. Although several important terms of the offer are missing from this statement (for instance, how long the offer will stay open), it's an unequivocal declaration that the seller will sell you the car at a specific price.

Once a legitimate offer has been made, it must be accepted. Telling the car seller above that you would buy his car for $1,495 wouldn't constitute an acceptance. Normally, the acceptance must be a carbon copy of the offer.

After an offer has been made and accepted, there must be consideration. In this context, "consideration" doesn't mean that admirable quality that your mother complained you never showed her; it means that each party must give up something of value. For instance, in the hypothetical car sale, the seller would have to give up his car, and you would have to give up $1,500 for the agreement to be considered valid.

In spite of the word's polite connotations, consideration doesn't have to be equal. If a seller makes a stupid deal and offers his car for sale at $100 when it's worth $1,500, this would normally still constitute sufficient consideration to create an enforceable contract. People have every right in the world to make bad deals. The law simply insists that each party give up something.

An offer, an acceptance of that offer, and consideration by both parties are the basics of a valid contract. Although it's easy to make a contract, if it involves an expensive item or an important deal, you may wish to run it by a lawyer, because there are a variety of ways to invalidate a contract. If the terms are too vague, for instance, a court might refuse to enforce it. A lawyer who specializes in contract law could help you protect yourself by making sure your contract is binding.

Although the rules regarding contracts may seem fairly simple, from the first days of *The People's Court* desperate litigants have pleaded with Judge Wapner to unravel the contractual webs they'd woven. Sometimes he could; other times he couldn't.

WHAT HAPPENS WHEN THERE ISN'T A SPECIFIC AGREEMENT ON PRICE?

Even if a contract has the minimal requirements for enforcement (offer, acceptance, and consideration), there are other reasons why jurists like Judge Wapner might not enforce them. The most common reason is the omission of essential terms. For instance, if you were to make a contract to buy widgets from a widget manufacturer, and you agreed to pay $1 per widget but forgot to specify the number of widgets that you were to purchase, a judge might well refuse to enforce the contract. In legalese, such a contract would be "indefinite as to the quantity term." That term is an essential element of a contract and must be explicitly stated.

Even if you agreed to buy "some" widgets from the widget manufacturer above, a court might rule that the term "some" is too indefinite and, therefore, that the contract is unenforceable.

Litigants sometimes argue that a judge is capable of filling in the missing terms of a contract. And in some cases a judge might agree to do so. If, for instance, two parties had been doing business under the same contract for six years in a row, and the seventh year a term was left out of their agreement, a judge might fill in that missing term. But this instance would be the exception rather than the rule. Judges are in the business of enforcing contracts, not redrafting them.

The most common defect in contracts is that the price term isn't specific enough. Parties often deliberately leave the price term vague because they're embarrassed or afraid to discuss money.

A judge ordinarily won't enforce an agreement in which the price term isn't specific. This can create problems, however, when one party fulfills obligations under the contract only to have the other party refuse to pay because the agreement is unenforceable. There's a legal doctrine that allows judges to "do justice" in such cases; it's called *quantum meruit,* or, in English, "reasonable value of services rendered." *People's Court* watchers probably know this term well, even if they never took those dreaded two years of Latin in high school.

One of the best illustrations of this doctrine on *The People's Court* was the case of "The Ski-Resort Snow Job." The plaintiff in this case claimed she'd made three stained-glass windows for the defendant in exchange for his promise that he would either pay her "the value of her services" or let her use his cabin at a local ski resort; however, once the windows were safely in their panes, the defendant refused to do either.

The defendant felt that, because he and the plaintiff had been romantically involved while she was making the windows, he shouldn't have to abide by the agreement. He felt that the windows were the spoils of love and had nothing to do with business.

Justice, however, is probably blinder than love. Judge Wapner didn't see what the parties' relationship had to do with their agreement. He saw only that the plaintiff had given the defendant something of value and was entitled to compensation.

It was true, explained the Judge, that in this case there was no specific price term. The defendant had only promised the use of the cabin or "the value of [the plaintiff's] services." But it was apparent from the testimony that the plaintiff hadn't been making a gift of her services and that the defendant had expected to give her some compensation. Before the plaintiff had begun work, the defendant could have disavowed the contract because the price term was indefinite. This would have left the plaintiff with no legal recourse. But the defendant had allowed the plaintiff to make the windows in spite of the vague price term. It would have been unfair to let the defendant get something for nothing because of a legal technicality.

Therefore, Judge Wapner decided to invoke the doctrine of *quantum meruit*. Judges have considerable discretion in determining what constitutes reasonable value. In some cases, they look at the going rate for the service that was performed; in other cases, they look at what the plaintiff in question would normally charge. In this case, the plaintiff gave the defendant two price options—the use of his cabin for a weekend or the value of the plaintiff's services. The plaintiff couldn't tell Judge Wapner what her services were worth, since she really didn't have a fixed price. Therefore, in the interest of justice, Judge Wapner awarded her the equivalent of one weekend's rent at the defendant's cabin—$300.

WHAT IF YOU'RE PRESSURED INTO SIGNING A CONTRACT?

Impulsive shoppers beware! A judge won't come to your rescue just because you're the victim of a slick sales pitch. If the salesman says, "This sofa will make your room," but when you get it home it only makes you sick, you might be out of luck. Buyer's remorse is no excuse for breaking a contract. So when a salesperson says you can't live without something, be sure that you can at least live with it before you agree to buy it.

There is, however, at least one situation in which you can break a contract. If the other party in a contract uses duress to get you to sign, you might be entitled to renege. Some state laws define "duress" as "a wrongful act which compels assent through fear." Often, duress involves *unlawful* confinement. If a salesman says, "I won't let you leave this room till you sign," and then locks the doors of the room until you deliver your John Hancock, consider yourself unlawfully confined and acting under duress. Similarly, if you sign because the other party in a contract says, "Sign or I'll have Big Louie and some o' de udder guys break your legs," a judge might feel you signed under duress. In other words, if you accept an offer because you literally can't refuse it, you might be able to get out of it.

In order to constitute duress, the pressure exerted on a party to enter an agreement must be drastic. Litigants sometimes mistakenly believe that extremely pushy sales pitches or other innocuous forms of intimidation constitute duress. In the case of "Battle at the Bike Shop," for example, the defendant sought

The plaintiff's son testifies in the case of
"The Battle at the Bike Shop."

to be exonerated from an agreement he'd made with the plaintiff on the grounds that the plaintiff had badgered him into entering it. Judge Wapner had to decide whether or not the plaintiff's badgering constituted duress.

The plaintiff in this case had bought a bicycle from the defendant's store, only to have it fall apart after several days. She said that when she'd returned it, the defendant told her to pick out another one; she picked out a cheaper model and the defendant handed her a receipt marked: "Balance due customer to be mailed—$28.57." The defendant later refused to pay this difference.

The defendant said that the bike the plaintiff had returned was damaged and that he'd decided to deduct the cost of repairing it from her refund; therefore, he claimed he owed her nothing.

The defendant also said that he wouldn't have made an

agreement to refund the difference in value between the two bikes in the first place if he hadn't been acting under duress. He explained that the plaintiff had returned the bike on a busy day just before Christmas and caused a great commotion in the store for nearly three hours. He'd written the receipt only out of exasperation, he said, and shouldn't be held to it.

But Judge Wapner didn't feel that the plaintiff's actions were severe enough to constitute duress. However obnoxious, there was nothing unlawful or even unscrupulous about the plaintiff's persistence. The defendant had made a deal and he was stuck with it, said the Judge. Judgment for the plaintiff.

Proving duress is very difficult, particularly in contract cases—as well it should be! After all, imagine the chaos that would ensue if everyone who felt remorse about a contract could wiggle out of it merely by saying, "He made me sign it." If you wish to rescind an agreement because you feel you were unlawfully coerced into it, consult a lawyer, who can help you decide whether or not you have a case and can advise you on how to present it most effectively.

WHAT ARE THE SPECIAL RULES GOVERNING CONTRACTS WITH MINORS?

The laws in many states allow minors to back out of many of the contracts they make. This lenient policy is designed to prevent business people from taking advantage of minors. After all, few minors have acquired the kind of bargaining skills that adults possess. Unscrupulous adults could easily prey on unsophisticated adolescents, binding them to bad deals.

Obviously, the effect of these laws is that adults are deterred from entering into contracts with minors; instead, they're encouraged to make contracts with parents or guardians.

There are a few exceptions to the leniency shown minors

regarding contracts. Most notably, minors typically can't "disaffirm" contracts for "necessities" such as food and shelter. Necessities don't include record albums and radios, popular adolescent opinion notwithstanding.

Also, if a minor makes a contract that isn't for a necessity and then uses the unnecessary product, the law doesn't allow him or her to rescind the deal scot-free. If a minor buys a car and uses it for three months before deciding to undo the deal, the law would allow the seller to retain a sum for depreciation. And, a minor might not be allowed to return a used item that has no resale value, such as a record album.

Not surprisingly, in the many states that have laws allowing minors to disaffirm contracts, many court cases arise on the subject. Since California has this law, *The People's Court* has hosted a few such disputes. "The Kid Who Couldn't," for instance, involved a fifteen-year-old plaintiff who bought a used car from the defendant for $185, used it for one month, then decided to return it, using his age as a reason for rescinding the purchase agreement.

The defendant, however, claimed that he'd had no way of knowing that the young man was a minor when he sold him the car. Furthermore, he contended that the car had been returned with a cracked drive shaft, which cost him $85 to repair.

The young plaintiff countered that during the month he'd owned the car, he'd added a battery and hoses. The defendant was getting the benefit of these enhancements free of charge, so why shouldn't he pay for the repairs?

Judge Wapner explained that since the car isn't a necessity of life, even in Southern California, the plaintiff was legally entitled to rescind the purchase because he was a minor—regardless of whether or not the defendant had known this at the time of the sale. However, the Judge explained that the plaintiff was liable for the amount of depreciation the car had incurred since he'd bought it. In this particular instance, the Judge felt that the plaintiff's improvements to the vehicle canceled out his damage. Therefore, Judge Wapner awarded the plaintiff a full refund.

Sometimes it's unclear whether the parent or the child is the actual party in an agreement. This was the situation in "If the Saddle Fits." The plaintiff was a thirteen-year-old girl who purchased a saddle from her friend's father, the defendant, for $300. The plaintiff's father, however, made out the check for the purchase. Later, the plaintiff decided that she wanted to return the saddle for a refund because it was old and worn.

The defendant admitted that the saddle was indeed seven years old and worn, but said he'd never represented it otherwise. He felt that since the plaintiff had known what she was buying, she shouldn't be allowed to change her mind.

Again, Judge Wapner explained that a minor may disaffirm a contract that isn't for the necessities of life. The case, however, was complicated by the fact that the plaintiff's father, not the plaintiff, had actually purchased the saddle; therefore, the plaintiff's father was the one who'd really entered into the agreement. So Judge Wapner held for the defendant, leaving the young plaintiff saddled with the saddle.

WHEN CAN YOU BREAK A CONTRACT?

Don't get excited by the title of this section. As we've seen, contracts aren't easy to break. In most cases, when you make a bad deal, you must chalk it up as tuition to the school of experience. You should always think long and hard before committing yourself to any kind of substantial agreement.

But there are instances less drastic than duress in which you may have legal justification for getting out of a deal. If you purchase a product that turns out to be nothing like what it was supposed to be, for example, you may be able to rescind the purchase agreement.

The case of "How Much Wood in the Old Oak Hutch?" was a good for-instance. The plaintiff bought a dining-room hutch from the defendant that was advertised in the newspaper as an oak hutch. When she got it home, however, the plaintiff found that the hutch was merely cleverly disguised plastic—certainly not destined to become a family heirloom. The plaintiff wanted to rescind the purchase contract and recover her real $150.

The defendant maintained she'd honestly thought the hutch was made of oak when she sold it. The things they can do with plastic these days! But a courtroom examination revealed the plaintiff was right—the oak was counterfeit.

Judge Wapner and Rusty examine the evidence in the case of "How Much Wood in the Old Oak Hutch?"

CONTRACTS: DOTTED-LINE DILEMMAS

Judge Wapner observed that *both* parties had thought that the hutch was oak. That, the judge said, was a "mutual mistake of fact." This mistake went to the essence of the contract. In the interest of justice, judges have the power to rescind contracts that have a mutual mistake at their core. And that was precisely what Judge Wapner did.

Thus, the plaintiff in this case recovered her money and the defendant recovered her plastic hutch.

A contract can also be repudiated if the other party is tardy in living up to his end of the deal. In most states, if the parties write into their agreement that "time is of the essence," then every second counts. When ordering a couch, for example, if you write on the invoice that time is of the essence and that the couch must be delivered on or before April 15, you may have a good case for repudiating the agreement if your social gathering on April 16 resembles a Japanese tea ceremony, with everyone sitting on the floor.

If, however, you don't indicate that time is important, you may not have an out if the other party should prove tardy in performing his duties under the contract; but if the person doesn't perform the obligations within a "reasonable" amount of time, then you could still break the agreement.

The case of "Bicycle Built for None" illustrates the issue of reasonable time. When the frame of the bike the plaintiff had bought from the defendant's store broke after a short time, the defendant assured her that the bicycle had a lifetime guarantee and that he would return it to the manufacturer and have it replaced; after five months of waiting impatiently for the replacement, however, the plaintiff finally bought another bike and filed suit against the defendant to recover the cost of the defective one—$263.33.

Judge Wapner explained that it was the defendant's responsibility to take care of problems within a reasonable

*The plaintiffs with their frameless bicycle in the case of
"The Bicycle Built for None."*

amount of time. Five months, he felt, was too long. Therefore, he ordered the defendant to reimburse the plaintiff.

You may also be entitled to get out of a deal when circumstances change in such a way that the contract completely loses its value. This legal doctrine is called frustration
of purpose. Under this doctrine, when both parties know the
purpose of a contract, and something happens after the
agreement is signed to make the contract worthless to one
party, then that party may be entitled to undo the deal.

The plaintiff in the case of "The Bandleader Who Wouldn't
Budge," for example, made an agreement with the defendant, a bandleader, to have his group play at her husband's
sixtieth birthday party. She gave the maestro a $100 deposit.

Tragically, the plaintiff's husband died before the party. The
plaintiff tried to break the agreement with the defendant, but
he said he would refund her deposit only if he got another

job on the day the party was supposed to take place.

Judge Wapner suggested that common sense was the best way to approach this case. The purpose of the contract—to provide entertainment at the husband's birthday party—had been made clear to the defendant at the time of the agreement. This purpose was rendered unattainable by the husband's death. Therefore, it should have been clear to the defendant that the purpose of the contract no longer existed and that the contract was worthless. Judge Wapner invalidated the agreement and ordered the defendant to refund the plaintiff's deposit.

Had the plaintiff not made the contract's purpose clear, she might have been out of luck. When making an agreement of this nature, always expressly state the reason for the deal; then, should circumstances change drastically, you might be able to cancel the arrangement.

There are circumstances other than the three above in which you might be entitled to back out of a contract. For the most part, however, contracts are binding. Just as it's sometimes worth your while to consult an attorney when formulating an important contract, it might also be worth your while sometimes to consult a lawyer when trying to get out of an important contract.

... TAKE 'EM TO COURT.

10

TO SUE OR
NOT TO SUE

Americans have become lawsuit crazy. The legal system is
looked to as a panacea for almost every kind of dispute life
has to offer. To be sure, many battles are worth fighting before a judge. But others should never see the inside of a
courtroom.

The People's Court has played host to many disputes that
should never have reached the hallowed halls of justice. For
instance, we've seen intrafamilial disagreements, such as who
owns Grandma's grandfather clock and who owns the fan in
the dining room, which should have been argued in the family kitchen over a cheese Danish. By and large, such petty
disputes are a waste of the court's time and the taxpayer's
money.

Small-claims courts are particularly plagued by cases that
don't require jurisprudence, because in most instances small-
claims cases are those not worth a lawyer's attention. After
all, the amount you can sue for in small-claims is limited in

every state (see Appendix), so it would be senseless to use a lawyer when the fees might easily exceed the amount of the judgment.

Fortunately, most big cities and many smaller ones have bar associations that provide lawyer referral services. Typically, these services allow you to meet with a lawyer for a low-cost consultation, usually less than $15. A thirty-minute meeting with a lawyer can help you determine the value of pursuing a dispute in court.

If you can't meet with a lawyer, or simply don't want to, there's another way to evaluate your claim: common sense. If you honestly believe you've been wronged—not emotionally, but actually—you probably have a legitimate case. This doesn't necessarily mean that you'll win, but you can at least feel confident that your case is worth fighting. Too often emotions stand in the way of accurately assessing the legitimacy of a dispute; the argument becomes so heated that clear thinking turns to steam and evaporates. Parties become so engrossed in the "principle" of an argument that they lose sight of its realities. Personal beliefs about what is right and wrong can obfuscate the merit of a claim.

For this reason, it's always—repeat, always—a good idea to run your problem by someone who doesn't have a stake in the outcome. If that person objectively evaluates your case and feels you've been done dirty, and that you can prove it, then maybe it's worth pursuing. Remember, you're not going to that person for a legal evaluation, but for a common-sense evaluation. Perhaps it's best to ask several people for their opinions. If everyone says you're fighting a petty war, or that your claim is unreasonable, then maybe you should listen.

Once you believe you have a valid claim, then you've reached step two, which is *not* going to court. You should *always* try to settle your dispute before filing suit. Many states require you to make an attempt to settle out of court. Some states, for instance, require you to make a demand for payment before suing a debtor; only if your demand goes unrequitted are you allowed to sue.

It's always better to settle out of court, regardless of how vindictive you feel toward the other party and how much you want to inconvenience him or her. Most judges can see right through a lawsuit that's brought for harassment purposes, and such motivations turn most judges off. They don't like to see the court's time wasted. If it's a close case and the judge doesn't like your approach, he or she just might rule against you because of it. This would put you in a far worse position than if you'd accepted a compromise solution.

Normally, the best way to negotiate a settlement is to make a demand in writing. Writing the demand is important, because the other party usually takes a written request more seriously than a verbal one.

Whether or not you should demand a specific sum of money depends on the situation. Although many negotiators try to press the other party to the wall, this isn't always a good strategy if you're serious about arriving at an out-of-court settlement. Making an unreasonable demand creates the risk of being flatly rejected, without a counteroffer.

If this happens, you might find yourself between a rock and a hard place. Should you make a second offer, lower than the first, this would probably be viewed as a sign of weakness. Therefore, it's always best to make an offer that you don't think will be rejected. At the same time, you should make an offer high enough to allow the other party some negotiating flexibility and still leave you with a satisfactory amount. In other words, your offer should be at the high end of the spectrum of reasonableness.

You must be serious about your case when you negotiate. Before you begin, decide what your bottom line is; then, *do not go below that line*. In other words, determine an amount below which you would rather take your chances in court. Some bottom lines may be "anything," and that's perfectly okay. But whatever your bottom line is, stick to it!

If negotiations prove futile, this doesn't mean you should run to the courthouse and file legal papers. You may still be able to resolve the dispute on your own and to your satisfaction. For instance, if the dispute involves a car accident and the other party won't pay your auto repair bills, you should review your insurance policy. If you have collision coverage, you may be able to file a claim with your insurance company. Of course, if there's a deductible, that amount would still come out of your pocket, and you might want to recoup it. Your insurance company might even help you do this by pursuing the claim against the other driver. The greatest advantage of this strategy is that insurance companies usually pay relatively quickly; you could pay most of the repair bill from the insurance proceeds, without having to advance much of the cost.

Another alternative to going to court is self-help, as discussed in the chapter on neighborhood disputes. Again, remember that self-help is only justified in limited situations, and if you abuse your right to use it, you could be sued. For instance, in disputes involving overhanging tree branches, some states allow you to cut the branches back to the property line, but if you cut further than that, you could be sued by the tree's owner if the tree is damaged as a result. Because self-help has only limited applications and is an approach that must be handled with caution, it's wise to consult a lawyer before employing it.

Also, some states offer mediation services, whereby a neutral mediator will try to resolve a dispute out of court. The mediator's problem, of course, is the same as yours—finding a solution that both sides can live with. But it can be done. One party's victory is not always the other's defeat. There are cases, many cases, in which a skilled mediator can send both parties away satisfied. Investigate to see if your area offers a mediation service.

If you do decide to sue, a major issue you must consider before filing is whether the other party can afford to pay the judgment if you prevail. The maxim "You can't squeeze blood from a turnip" shouldn't be ignored. Rough estimates are that more than 30 percent of small-claims-court judgments go uncollected because the other party can't pay. If your adversary isn't solvent, it might not be worth the expense and inconvenience of going to court.

However, before dismissing the other party because of financial status, you should take into account that judgments in most states are enforceable for up to ten years. The pauper who dents your fender could turn out to be a regular Horatio Alger. Five years later, when he's chairman of the board of a multimillion-dollar corporation, you could enforce your judgment. Justice might be delayed, but it wouldn't be denied.

Furthermore, some states allow you to extend a judgment even beyond ten years. Therefore, if there's any chance that the person you're considering taking to court could someday have assets, it may be worthwhile.

If the other party is a minor, remember that when a minor does the dirty deed, you may have a good case not only against him, but against his parents as well (see "Neighborhood Feuds"). In many states, parents are liable for the willful misconduct of their minor children. Parents could even be liable when their minors are guilty of negligent driving, if they implicitly gave their children permission to drive. So, even if the minor isn't making money, you might still be able to sue and collect from his parents.

When deciding whom to sue in any case, be sure to include all the people who may be liable for the damage you're alleging. If you file suit against all those who appear to be responsible, you stand a better chance of collecting your judgment, because even if one person can't pay, you can still go after the others.

Caution: Don't sue everyone under the sun. If you sue someone and there's no basis for bringing him or her to court, you could find yourself on the other side of justice's scales—the defendant's side. If the person you sued without any cause prevails, he or she could turn around and file suit against you for malicious prosecution. So choose your defendants carefully.

Another thing to consider when filing a suit is the statute of limitations. Even if you have a claim that appears to be valid—in other words, if you can prove negligence or that someone breached a contract—your case may still be thrown out of court if you wait too long to act. Every state imposes time limits for filing suits. They vary from state to state, but most states impose a two-year limit for filing against someone who breaches an oral contract and a four-year limit for filing against someone who breaches a written contract. And when you're suing for personal injuries caused by negligence, many states require that you file suit within one year of the injury. If you don't file within the required period, you could lose your day in court despite the validity of your claim. Therefore, if there's any concern, you should check with a lawyer to make sure you haven't run afoul of the statute of limitations.

11

PREPARING FOR COURT

It's often said that winning is 1 percent perspiration and 99 percent preparation. Certainly this ratio holds true for winning a legal case.

In most courts, but particularly in small-claims courts, litigants constantly amaze judges with their widely divergent accounts of what happened. How can two people who presumably witnessed the same event recount such different stories? So many litigants seem to be singing the Gershwin duet that goes:

> You say tomato, I say tomahto.
> You say potato, I say potahto.
> Tomato, tomahto,
> Potato, potahto,

that Judge Wapner must often feel like calling the whole thing off.

THE PEOPLE'S COURT

Of course, the conflicting songs and dances of litigants are inspired by the desire to win the case. And, obviously, a litigant who can make his case more than simply a matter of his word against his adversary's will have a substantial edge. In other words, tell the judge *why* you say potahto.

This edge is especially important when you're the person filing suit. Generally (but not always) the person who asserts a claim has the burden of proof, meaning that he must prove that his story is more plausible than the other party's. You don't have to overwhelm your adversary to win; tipping the scales ever so slightly will do. The formula is roughly that you must prove your case by 50.000001 percent.

If it's a simple standoff—that is, if it's your word against his—and you have the burden of proof, you may have problems. The judge can consider the credibility of both parties, and if the judge believes that your credibility is in doubt, you could lose the case. If the judge simply doesn't know whom to believe, and you have the burden of proof, you would normally lose.

Thus, it's of the utmost importance to arrive in court armed with enough evidence to meet your burden of proof or to undermine the case of the party who has the burden.

The evidence you'll need depends on the type of case. If the dispute involves payment of a debt, then contracts, canceled checks, bank statements, and anything else that can prove either payment or nonpayment will be critical. Regardless of whether you're the debtor or the creditor, *never pay or receive money in cash unless it's accompanied by a receipt and written proof of payment.* You should always make payments by check or money order; then, if a dispute ever arises, you'll have ready proof of payment.

Too many people make the mistake of thinking that their creditors would *never* sue, and thus that it's fine to pay them in cash. In fact, most litigants say they felt this way at the time of the transaction that landed them in court. This probably isn't due as much to naïveté as to the fact that very few people knowingly enter into a transaction with a schnook. In a world in which smiling, glad-handing schnooks abound, show foresight and make sure you have a record of who paid what to whom. Pay by check and, when possible, get a receipt.

Also, if you're fighting over a defective product, you should bring the product in question to court—along with the sales contract, proof of payment, and any other documents associated with the transaction.

If you're fighting over a service that you believe wasn't performed satisfactorily, you need to prove it. If the service was rendered on an object that can be brought to court, bring it along. The judge wants to see it firsthand.

If the object is so large that it isn't practical to bring it to court, then take pictures. Take *good* pictures that graphically show the defects you're citing.

Often, when you're suing over defective services, the person you're suing will hold that he or she is an expert. To counter your opponent's testimony, it may be necessary for you to be armed with your own expert, someone who can rebut the assertions. For instance, if you're suing a dry cleaner, you may need to get your own expert launderer to prove that the defendant left you hung out to dry.

Typically, it's not practical, or even possible, to bring your own expert to small-claims court. Either the expert is too busy or demands a fee that would eat up your judgment. Some states allow you to subpoena experts for the cost of a witness fee, and that fee may be modest enough to justify the expense. The problem, of course, is that you don't want to anger your expert. Someone who's dragged to court against his will may not do the best job for you. In recognition of this problem, many small-claims courts allow litigants to produce notarized statements. For instance, a dry cleaner could write a statement that says he has evaluated the garment in question and that it's obvious to him from his fifty-five years of experience that the dry cleaners in question used too much heat in the ironing process. Assuming the statement is honest, credible, and notarized, some judges will consider it. Realize, however, that written statements are only second best to live testimony, since the expert isn't in court to be cross-examined by the other party and observed by the judge. Nevertheless, many small-claims-court judges will consider notarized statements.

If the case involves personal injuries, you should bring along medical evidence of your injury (see the chapter on personal injuries). As explained above, reports and doctors' bills are vital. Furthermore, you may be able to sue for medical expenses you'll incur after your appearance in court, but only if you submit evidence substantiating the need and the cost of future treatment. For example, a letter from your doctor that states you'll need a minor operation to cure the problem at issue in the case and that quotes the price of the surgery will probably suffice.

If you lost wages as a result of an injury, bring proof to court. A letter from your employer would probably be sufficient. As you've already read, you cannot collect lost wages for the time you had to spend preparing your case and coming to court. You're only entitled to wages lost directly as a result of an injury. For instance, if someone negligently broke your leg and you were laid up for two weeks without pay as a result, then you might be able to collect two weeks' worth of wages.

Another important element of personal injury cases is pain and suffering—the pain, trauma, emotional distress, anguish, and ordeal associated with your injury. As discussed previously, judges have considerable discretion in awarding damages for pain and suffering, and you stand the best chance of collecting such damages if you can present proof that you suffered as a result of an injury. An effective way of proving this is by keeping a diary while you're experiencing pain and suffering. Entries should be made every time you feel discomfort as a result of the injury. Take your diary to bed and record every throb, however minor. Date each entry and note the time of day. Be as graphic as possible; this is one situation in which your bellyaching might pay off. The cumulative effect of the entries may be the most effective way of producing a sizable pain-and-suffering award.

When a personal injury case involves intentional misconduct, many small-claims courts have the power to award punitive damages, which serve as punishment. Normally, punitive damages aren't awarded in cases involving breach of contract. Also, if the wrongdoer simply acted imprudently or negligently, then the judge probably wouldn't award the victim punitive damages. But when there's evidence of willfulness or extreme recklessness on the culprit's part, then the judge might award punitive damages if he has the legal power in his jurisdiction.

If punitive damages are allowed, the amount of the award could vary considerably, depending on the financial status of the guilty party. Punitive damages are designed to deter the wrongdoer from committing similar actions in the future, and what it takes to deter one person may not be the same as what it takes to deter another. Thus, a rich person or a large company might have to pay five times what a poor person would have to pay before feeling the pinch and getting the message.

Although punitive damages are often awarded in proportion to the other damages, this normally isn't a requirement.

Therefore, if you have provable medical damages of only $100, a judge could still theoretically award $1,000 in punitive damages—or even more.

If you think you're entitled to punitive damages, you must usually ask for them. It's a good idea to make the request on the small-claims-court form you file.

If your case involves a car accident, you may wish to prepare a diagram on a large poster. This will help the judge follow your case, and it's important that the judge understand what you're saying at all times. The minute you lose the judge in a verbal fog, you jeopardize your case. A diagram is an effective tool for presenting a clear case.

If you're suing for repair costs, bring at least two estimates. Some judges require three, so you should probably get three estimates just to be on the safe side. Ordinarily, the judge will award you the lowest of the three estimates.

If you're the defendant in a case involving car repairs, you could try to get your own estimate of the plaintiff's damage. Of course, this would be impossible if the plaintiff denied you access to his car. Nevertheless, several general statements from auto repair shops ballparking the repair costs could influence the judge if the plaintiff estimates seem unduly high.

If you're the plaintiff, bring pictures of your damage to court. Make sure the photos are of sufficient quality to highlight the damage. There's nothing worse than showing a picture to a judge and having him tell you he can't see anything wrong.

In all cases, make sure that you can back up your claims. If the dispute centers around who saw what, the key is to get good witnesses. Again, if the witnesses cannot or will not show up in court, the judge may consider notarized statements.

Finally, common sense should lead you to much of the evidence that you'll need to prove your case, or disprove your adversary's case. It's better to bring too much evidence than not enough.

12

GOING TO COURT: DOS AND DON'TS

Although judges want, and in some cases demand, documentation, the litigant with the most witnesses and papers doesn't necessarily win the case. In court, as in a great restaurant, it's not just the ingredients, it's the presentation.

Not that you're expected to handle your case like Clarence Darrow; indeed, trying to do so will probably only get you into trouble. The key to effective presentation isn't polish but persuasiveness. And the secret to being persuasive is presenting a clear, simple, *understandable* case that makes your position appear reasonable and fair.

You aren't expected to speak like a lawyer; no Latin terms or jurisprudential banter is required. You should merely present a concise version of your side of the dispute in plain, simple English.

You should organize your presentation so the judge can follow it at all times. If your argument sounds confusing at any point, don't kid yourself that you'll be able to clear it up

193

later; the truth is that you run the risk of having the judge tune out when things become difficult to follow. After all, judges are human beings. They try to understand, but, black robes notwithstanding, their eyes sometimes glaze over during a muddled story just as yours do.

You should take to court an outline of the major points you want to make in your argument. By the time you pass through the double doors, you should have practiced your argument several times so you know that it makes sense and is reasonably concise. However, *you should not read a speech to the judge*—it's boring. No one likes listening to a prepared text. You can be far more effective, sincere, and convincing if it sounds like you're talking, not reading. If it takes more than a couple of three-by-five index cards to write your major points on, you're writing too much. Confine yourself to just the *major* points, just the facts.

Even if you're well organized, you won't do well if you're obnoxious. Most judges become quickly irritated by litigants who refuse to let their adversaries have their day in court. Similarly, judges aren't amused by sarcastic facial expressions and remarks designed to discredit your opponent. Even if you know the other party is a liar, don't say it outright. It's much more effective and less obnoxious to present a case that leads the judge to that conclusion.

And do not argue with your adversary. The time for arguing ends when you enter the courtroom. You should address the judge and only the judge. Small-claims-court judges are swayed more by facts than by arguments, and the difference can sometimes be subtle. It's more persuasive to say to a judge, "When I purchased the car the salesman told me that it had a new engine," than to tell him, "I would have been out of my mind to buy a five-thousand-dollar used car if I knew it had a dying engine." Again, you should present enough facts so that the conclusion seems almost inescapable. But let the judge draw the conclusion; you just provide the support.

Listen for signals. If the judge sounds like he's siding with you—if it sounds like you're winning and the other person is on the defensive—the smartest strategy might be silence. If you know you have the case in the bag, and the judge asks if you want to add anything, don't court disaster: Say no.

Don't bring too many witnesses. Limit yourself to only the ones who enhance your case. On occasion, cumulative witnesses can be important, but more often they don't add much. If the case turns on a critical conversation and you have two witnesses to that conversation, then you might want to ask both to appear on your behalf. But you can generally do without witnesses whose testimony is only peripheral to the case. Consider the judge, who has a docket of cases that must be completed within a short duration. Don't alienate him by wasting his valuable time.

Make sure your documentation is well organized. When the judge asks for a particular document, it should be at your fingertips. Disorganization can actually hurt the credibility of your case.

It's critical that you answer the questions the judge asks. If you begin your argument and the judge interrupts with a question, stop and answer it before proceeding with the rest of your story—even if it breaks the flow of your argument. If you brush off the judge by saying, "I'll get to that," you'll antagonize him. Never forget that you're trying to influence the judge. No matter how important you believe to be the order in which you're relating your story, should the judge want something different, defer to him. After all, it's he who's deciding the case; and if he thinks a point is important, then it is.

Pleasing the judge doesn't mean being an apple polisher. Don't compliment the judge on his or her robe, hair, tie, blouse, or anything else. Keep it strictly business.

You aren't expected to make a grand entrance in an Italian designer suit or a Christian Dior gown. Small-claims court is the people's court, not Joan Collins's. It's designed for working people who have day-to-day legal problems they can't resolve. It's fine to show up in working clothes, as long as they're neat and clean. T-shirts and torn jeans are discouraged, but if the nature of your work and your work schedule make them unavoidable, the judge should understand.

Don't wear hats or sunglasses. Judges want to evaluate your credibility, and that's hard to do when your face is barely visible. Also, don't chew gum; it's rude.

You should always provide the judge with a list of your expenses—court costs, the cost of serving papers on your adversary, witness fees, and so on. Depending on your financial status, you could recover some or all of these costs if you win.

If you're being sued and you lose, you can ask the judge for permission to pay in installments if you're strapped for cash.

13

ENFORCING
A JUDGMENT

If you win your case, you'll probably expect your fallen adversary to graciously pay you for your just due; unfortunately, it doesn't always happen that way. For one thing, losing parties sometimes appeal their cases, and judgments usually can't be enforced until all appeals have run their course. However, losers often just decide not to pay. Indeed, statistics show that as many as 30 percent of small-claims-court judgments go uncollected in some states.

There are several reasons why losers don't ante up. First, some people just don't have the money. Like the proverbial turnip, they have nothing to squeeze out. But don't forget that judgments can be good for many years; keep tabs on your debtor's financial status.

For others, it's a matter not of turnips, but of sour grapes.

In either case, the winning party ordinarily has to give the loser a certain amount of time, usually twenty days, before he can take action. And before any official action can be taken, the losing party should be notified, perferably in writing, that if the judgment isn't paid, further legal action will be initiated.

Some states allow the winner to subpoena the loser back to court. There, in an informal proceeding, usually without the presence of a judge, the winner can question the loser about his assets—his house, his car, his investments. The winner can also request the location of the assets and an accounting of what's owed on each. Information about checking and savings accounts are also fair game.

The loser usually must supply all this information under oath. If he lies, the judge could cite him with contempt of court or refer the matter for prosecution of perjury. This is usually enough incentive to inspire the loser to tell the truth.

If the loser refuses to answer the questions, the winner can ask the clerk of the court to get the judge. The parties could be ordered to go to the courtroom, where the judge would order the loser to answer all appropriate questions.

Once the prevailing party learns about the loser's assets, then some of those assets could be used to satisfy the judgment. Most states protect certain assets from being seized, such as furniture, clothing, a portion of the loser's bank and savings accounts, the family car, and the house.

Nevertheless, much can be taken to satisfy a judgment. Even if a portion of the loser's bank account is protected, the balance may be confiscated. Similarly, a portion of the loser's wages may be garnisheed (seized to satisfy the judgment).

Procedures vary for confiscating property or money to satisfy a judgment. Your local marshal should know what can be seized and should have the necessary forms to enable you to do it.

Interestingly, many losers who initially refuse to pay suddenly become cooperative when they realize the winner means business. Once the loser gets wind that the winner is going after certain assets, the loser may quickly decide to cooperate.

If you prevail against a business, you might have additional rights if the business owner refuses to pay the judgment. Many states allow the winner to have a marshal go to the place of business and stand by the cash register; as money comes in, the marshal can seize it to satisfy the judgment. This is called putting a keeper in the place of business. The marshal's cost of serving as a keeper is usually added on to the judgment, so the loser ends up paying that too.

Some states have another interesting way of enforcing a judgment against an uncooperative business. It's called a till tap: The marshal arrives at the business unannounced and demands everything in the cash drawer. This is quicker than using a keeper, but can only be done when there's some type of cash drawer present, or a reasonable facsimile.

When it comes to enforcing a judgment against a business, the embarrassment factor is often compelling. The last thing the business needs for public relations is a marshal coming to the store and making it look like the business is doing something wrong. Not surprisingly, therefore, most businesses would rather comply than endure this.

Before going through the process of enforcing a judgment, you need advice on how it works. It can get very technical, sometimes tricky. Therefore you should make sure you know what you're doing before you start. Check with the marshal and, if necessary, the court clerk. If they don't give you straight answers, call your bar association and ask for a low-cost consultation with a trial lawyer.

The key to enforcing a judgment is making it clear that you mean business. Once the loser knows that, he might just comply without your having to take further action.

AFTERWORD

If you have read this book cover to cover, you've probably learned a lot about your legal rights. Now that you're a legal scholar of sorts, you must decide what you'll do with your knowledge.

Too many people, lawyers included, are eager to file a lawsuit at the drop of a hat. These people think of a lawsuit as the first step toward solving a legal problem. In fact, a lawsuit should be the last step.

There are a multitude of ways legal disputes can be resolved short of going to court. Many cities offer mediation services in which a mediator works with parties embroiled in a dispute in an effort to find a solution satisfactory to both sides.

Many cities and states have established agencies to help consumers resolve disputes, especially those involving unfair business practices.

Perhaps the most effective way to resolve a dispute is to

AFTERWORD

confront your adversary directly. If you have the law on your side and you can prove it, your opponent may be willing to work toward a solution to the problem.

Lawsuits can be costly (remember, if you take time off work to appear in court, lost wages aren't recoverable) and emotionally upsetting, win or lose.

Our society has accepted preventive medicine. Why not preventive law? The next time you're having a legal problem, think of a solution, not a lawsuit. Your knowledge, along with some tact, could help you lead a happier life.

A NATIONAL SURVEY OF SMALL-CLAIMS COURTS

ALABAMA

Claim Limit: $500
Representation by Attorney: Permitted
Filing Cost: $22
Length of Case Backlog: Approximately one month
Judges' Powers: Award money damages. Judges also have certain equitable powers, such as ordering the return of property.
Appeal: Both plaintiff and defendant have right of appeal

ALASKA

Claim limit: $2,000
Representation by Attorney: Permitted
Filing Cost: $5
Length of Case Backlog: Approximately three weeks

Judges' Powers: Award money damages. Judges also have certain equitable powers, such as ordering enforcement of contracts.

Appeal: Both plaintiff and defendant have a right of appeal for disputes involving more than $50.

ARIZONA

Claim Limit: $2,500

Representation by Attorney: Permitted

Filing Cost: Between $1 and $10, depending on amount of claim

Length of Case Backlog: Approximately sixty days

Judges' Powers: Award money damages. Judges also have equitable powers, such as ordering parties to carry out the terms of a contract

Appeal: Both plaintiff and defendant can appeal adverse judgment that exceeds $20.

ARKANSAS

Claim Limit: Property Damage Claims—$100. Others—$300

Representation by Attorney: Permitted only for defendant

Filing Cost: $11.25

Length of Case Backlog: Approximately one month

Judges' Powers: Award money damages. Judges also have certain equitable powers, such as ordering enforcement of contracts.

Appeal: Both plaintiff and defendant may appeal

CALIFORNIA

Claim Limit: $1,500
Representation by Attorney: Not permitted
Filing Cost: $6
Length of Case Backlog: Approximately forty days
Judges' Powers: Award money damages. Judges also have certain equitable powers, such as ordering enforcement of a contract and ordering restitution
Appeal: Defendant may appeal plaintiff's claim. Plaintiff may appeal defendant's counter-suit

COLORADO

Claim Limit: $1,000
Representation by Attorney: Not permitted
Filing Cost: $8
Length of Case Backlog: Approximately sixty days
Judges' Power: Award money damages.
Appeal: Both plaintiff and defendant have a right of appeal

CONNECTICUT

Claim Limit: $1,000
Representation by Attorney: Permitted
Filing Cost: $20
Length of Case Backlog: Approximately one month
Judges' Power: Award money damages.
Appeal: Not permitted

DELAWARE

Claim Limit: $1,500
Representation by Attorney: Permitted

SURVEY OF SMALL-CLAIMS COURTS

Filing Cost: Between $16 and $21, depending on
claim
Length of Case Backlog: Approximately twenty-five
days
Judges' Powers: Award money damages. Judges also
have equitable powers, such as ordering enforcement of contracts
Appeal: Both plaintiff and defendant may appeal

FLORIDA

Claim Limit: $1,500
Representation by Attorney: Permitted
Filing Cost: Between $12 and $31, depending on
claim
Length of Case Backlog: Approximately six weeks
Judges' Power: Award money damages
Appeal: Both plaintiff and defendant may appeal

GEORGIA

Small-claims court abolished July 1983

HAWAII

Claim Limit: $2,500
Representation by Attorney: Permitted in all cases
except those involv-
ing a tenant's security
deposit
Filing Cost: $5
Length of Case Backlog: Approximately thirty days
Judges' Power: Award money damages
Appeal: Not permitted

IDAHO

Claim Limit: $2,000
Representation by Attorneys: Not permitted
Filing Cost: $28
Length of Case Backlog: Approximately three months
Judges' Power: Award money damages
Appeal: Both plaintiff and defendant may appeal

ILLINOIS

Claim Limit: $2,500 or less, depending on county
Representation by Attorney: Permitted
Filing Cost: Between $12 and $27, depending on amount of claim
Length of Case Backlog: Approximately three weeks
Judges' Power: Award money damages
Appeal: Both plaintiff and defendant may appeal

INDIANA

Claim Limit: $3,000
Representation by Attorney: Permitted
Filing Cost: Between $27 and $48, depending on amount of claim
Length of Case Backlog: Approximately three weeks
Judges' Powers: Award money damages. Judges also have certain equitable powers, such as ordering the return of property
Appeal: Permitted

IOWA:

Claim Limit: $2,000
Representation by Attorney: Permitted
Filing Cost: $11

SURVEY OF SMALL-CLAIMS COURTS

Length of Case Backlog: Approximately six weeks
Judges' Powers: Award money damages. Judges
               may also hear eviction cases
Appeal: Both plaintiff and defendant may appeal

KANSAS

Claim Limit: $500
Representation by Attorney: Not permitted
Filing Cost: $10
Length of Case Backlog: Approximately three weeks
Judges' Powers: Award money damages. Judges also
               have certain equitable powers, such
               as ordering the return of property
Appeal: Both plaintiff and defendant may appeal

KENTUCKY

Claim Limit: $1,000
Representation by Attorney: Permitted
Filing Cost: Approximately $19 (varies)
Length of Case Backlog: Approximately five weeks
Judges' Power: Award money damages
Appeal: Both plaintiff and defendant may appeal

LOUISIANA

Claim Limit: Generally $1,500 (varies by parrish)
Representation by Attorney: Permitted
Filing Cost: $15
Length of Case Backlog: Approximately four weeks
Judges' Powers: Award money damages. Judges also
               have certain equitable powers, such
               as ordering the return of property
Appeal: Not permitted

MAINE

Claim Limit: $1,000
Representation by Attorney: Permitted
Filing Cost: $10
Length of Case Backlog: Approximately two months
Judges' Powers: Award money damages. Judges also have certain equitable powers, including ordering the enforcement of contracts
Appeal: Both plaintiff and defendant may appeal

MARYLAND

Claim Limit: $1,000
Representation by Attorney: Permitted
Filing Cost: $5
Length of Case Backlog: Approximately seven weeks
Judges' Power: Award money damages
Appeal: Both plaintiff and defendant may appeal

MASSACHUSETTS

Claim Limit: $1,200
Representation by Attorney: Permitted
Filing Cost: Between $8.75 and $12.75, depending on amount of claim
Length of Case Backlog: Approximately five weeks
Judges' Power: Award money damages
Appeal: Defendant may appeal plaintiff's claim. Plaintiff may appeal defendant's counter-suit

MICHIGAN

Claim Limit: $600
Representation by Attorney: Not permitted

Filing Cost: Between $5 and $6, depending on amount of claim
Length of Case Backlog: Approximately three weeks
Judges' Power: Award money damages
Appeal: Not permitted

MINNESOTA

Claim Limit: $1,250
Representation by Attorney: Not permitted
Filing Cost: Between $5 and $15, depending on amount of claim
Length of Case Backlog: Approximately one month
Judges' Powers: Award money damages. Judges also have certain equitable powers, such as ordering the return of property
Appeal: Both plaintiff and defendant may appeal

MISSISSIPPI

Claim Limit: $1,000
Representation by Attorney: Permitted
Filing Cost: $26 minimum
Length of Case Backlog: Approximately two weeks
Judges' Powers: Award money damages. Judges also have certain equitable powers, such as ordering enforcement of contracts
Appeal: Both plaintiff and defendant may appeal

MISSOURI

Claim Limit: $1,000
Representation by Attorney: Permitted
Filing Cost: Between $5 and $10, depending on amount of claim
Length of Case Backlog: Approximately three weeks

Judges' Power: Award money damages
Appeal: Both plaintiff and defendant may appeal

MONTANA

Claim Limit: $1,500
Representation by Attorney: Not permitted
Filing Cost: $5
Length of Case Backlog: Approximately two weeks
Judges' Power: Award money damages
Appeal: Both plaintiff and defendant may appeal

NEBRASKA

Claim Limit: $1,000
Representation by Attorney: Not permitted
Filing Cost: $6
Length of Case Backlog: Approximately one month
Judges' Powers: Award money damages. Judges also have certain equitable powers, including ordering enforcement of contracts
Appeal: Both plaintiff and defendant may appeal

NEVADA

Claim Limit: $1,000
Representation by Attorney: Permitted
Filing Cost: Between $20 and $30, depending on amount of claim
Length of Case Backlog: Approximately three months
Judges' Powers: Award money damages. Judges also have certain equitable powers, such as ordering the return of property
Appeal: Both plaintiff and defendant may appeal

NEW HAMPSHIRE

Claim Limit: $1,500
Representation by Attorney: Permitted
Filing Cost: $10
Length of Case Backlog: Approximately two months
Judges' Powers: Award money damages. Judges also have certain equitable powers, such as ordering the return of property
Appeal: Allowed only in limited cases

NEW JERSEY

Claim Limit: $1,000
Representation by Attorney: Permitted
Filing Cost: $4.10
Length of Case Backlog: Approximately three weeks
Judges' Power: Award money damages
Appeal: Both plaintiff and defendant may appeal

NEW MEXICO

Claim Limit: $2,000
Representation by Attorney: Permitted
Filing Cost: $10
Length of Case Backlog: Approximately one month
Judges' Power: Award money damages
Appeal: Both plaintiff and defendant may appeal

NEW YORK

Claim Limit: $1,500
Representation by Attorney: Permitted
Filing Cost: $3
Length of Case Backlog: Approximately one month
Judges' Powers: Award money damages. Judges also have certain equitable powers, such as ordering the return of property

Appeal: Defendant may appeal adverse ruling. Plaintiff may appeal only on grounds of "substantial injustice"

NORTH CAROLINA

Claim Limit: $1,000
Representation by Attorney: Permitted
Filing Cost: $15
Length of Case Backlog: Approximately one month
Judges' Power: Award money damages
Appeal: Both plaintiff and defendant may appeal

NORTH DAKOTA

Claim Limit: $1,500
Representation by Attorney: Permitted
Filing Cost: $6
Length of Case Backlog: Approximately one month
Judges' Power: Award money damages
Appeal: Not permitted

OHIO

Claim Limit: $1,000
Representation by Attorney: Permitted
Filing Cost: Between $6 and $20, depending on amount of claim
Length of Case Backlog: Approximately one month
Judges' Power: Award money damages
Appeal: Both plaintiff and defendant may appeal

OKLAHOMA

Claim Limit: $1,500
Representation by Attorney: Permitted
Filing Cost: $25

Length of Case Backlog: Approximately three weeks
Judges' Powers: Award money damages. Judges also
        have certain equitable powers, such
        as ordering the return of property
Appeal: Both plaintiff and defendant may appeal

OREGON

Claim Limit: $1,000
Representation by Attorney: Not permitted, except
        with judge's consent
Filing Cost: $33.60
Length of Case Backlog: Approximately one month
Judges' Powers: Award money damages. Judges also
        have certain equitable powers, such
        as ordering the enforcement of
        contracts
Appeal: Not permitted

PENNSYLVANIA

Claim Limit: $4,000
Representation by Attorney: Permitted. Judge has
        power to order rep-
        resentation by attor-
        ney
Filing Cost: $5
Length of Case Backlog: Approximately two weeks
Judges' Power: Award money damages
Appeal: Both plaintiff and defendant may appeal

RHODE ISLAND

Claim Limit: $1,000
Representation by Attorney: Permitted
Filing Cost: $5
Length of Case Backlog: Approximately one month

THE PEOPLE'S COURT

Judges' Power: Award money damages
Appeal: Defendant may appeal plaintiff's claim. Plaintiff may appeal defendant's counter-suit.

SOUTH CAROLINA

Claim Limit: $1,000
Representation by Attorney: Permitted
Filing Cost: $15
Length of Case Backlog: Approximately six weeks
Judges' Powers: Award money damages. Judges also have certain equitable powers, such as ordering the return of property
Appeal: Both plaintiff and defendant may appeal

SOUTH DAKOTA

Claim Limit: $2,000
Representation by Attorney: Permitted
Filing Cost: Between $6.75 and $22.75, depending on amount of claim
Length of Case Backlog: Approximately five weeks
Judges' Power: Award money damages
Appeal: Not permitted

TENNESSEE

Claim Limit: $10,000 and up, depending on the county
Representation by Attorney: Permitted
Filing Cost: $32.75
Length of Case Backlog: Approximately one month
Judges' Powers: Award money damages. Judges also have certain equitable powers, such

as ordering enforcement of contracts
Appeal: Both plaintiff and defendant may appeal

TEXAS

Claim Limit: $1,000
Representation by Attorney: Permitted
Filing Cost: $27
Length of Case Backlog: Approximately three weeks
Judges' Power: Award money damages
Appeal: Both plaintiff and defendant may appeal

UTAH

Claim Limit: $600
Representation by Attorney: Permitted
Filing Cost: $12.50
Length of Case Backlog: Approximately twenty days
Judges' Power: Award money damages
Appeal: Defendant may appeal plaintiff's claim.
Plaintiff may appeal defendant's counter-
suit

VERMONT

Claim Limit: $2,000
Representation by Attorney: Permitted
Filing Cost: $10
Length of Case Backlog: Approximately two months
Judges' Powers: Award money damages. Judges also
have certain equitable powers, such
as ordering the return of property
Appeal: Both plaintiff and defendant may appeal

VIRGINIA

Claim Limit: $7,000
Representation by Attorney: Permitted
Filing Cost: $8.50
Length of Case Backlog: Approximately two weeks
Judges' Power: Award money damages
Appeal: Both plaintiff and defendant may appeal
cases involving more than $50

WASHINGTON STATE

Claim Limit: $1,000
Representation by Attorney: Not permitted without judge's consent
Filing Cost: $10
Length of Case Backlog: Approximately one month
Judges' Power: Award money damages
Appeal: Defendant may appeal

WASHINGTON, D.C.

Claim Limit: $750
Representation by Attorney: Permitted
Filing Cost: $1
Length of Case Backlog: Approximately two weeks
Judges' Power: Award money damages
Appeal: Both plaintiff and defendant may appeal

WEST VIRGINIA

Claim Limit: $2,000
Representation by Attorney: Permitted
Filing Cost: $10
Length of Case Backlog: Approximately one month
Judges' Powers: Award money damages. Judges also

have certain equitable powers, such
as ordering the return of property
Appeal: Both plaintiff and defendant may appeal

WISCONSIN

Claim Limit: $1,000
Representation by Attorney: Permitted
Filing Cost: $12
Length of Case Backlog: Approximately two weeks
Judges' Powers: Award money damages. Judges also
have certain equitable powers, in-
cluding ordering the return of
property
Appeal: Both plaintiff and defendant may appeal

WYOMING

Claim Limit: $750
Representation by Attorney: Permitted
Filing Cost: $2
Length of Case Backlog: Approximately two weeks
Judges' Powers: Award money damages. Judges also
have certain equitable powers, in-
cluding ordering the enforcement
of contracts
Appeal: Both plaintiff and defendant may appeal

About the Author

Harvey Levin is the legal consultant to *The People's Court.*
For KNBC in Los Angeles, he is a legal reporter and the host
of *Headlines on Trial.* Mr. Levin also interprets the law in a
Los Angeles Times weekly column called "The Law and You"
and in regular segments on *Hour Magazine.*

A graduate of the University of Chicago Law School, he is
a member of the State Bar of California.

Mr. Levin lives in Hollywood Hills.

Judge Wapner with the staff of The People's Court.
The show is produced by Ralph Edwards Productions
in association with Stu Billett Productions.

INDEX

INDEX

INDEX

INDEX

223

INDEX

224